SOUTH AF~~RICAN ART~~

IN STONE

&

PAINT

SOUTH AFRICA'S PAST
IN STONE
&
PAINT

By

M. C. BURKITT, M.A., F.S.A., F.G.S.

University Lecturer at Cambridge in the Faculty of
Archaeology and Anthropology

Author of

Prehistory, Our Forerunners,
Our Early Ancestors,
etc.

CAMBRIDGE

AT THE UNIVERSITY PRESS

1928

CAMBRIDGE UNIVERSITY PRESS
Cambridge, New York, Melbourne, Madrid, Cape Town,
Singapore, São Paulo, Delhi, Tokyo, Mexico City

Cambridge University Press
The Edinburgh Building, Cambridge CB2 8RU, UK

Published in the United States of America by Cambridge University Press, New York

www.cambridge.org
Information on this title: www.cambridge.org/9781107641334

First published 1928
First paperback edition 2011

A catalogue record for this publication is available from the British Library

ISBN 978-1-107-64133-4 Paperback

To

SIR CARRUTHERS BEATTIE

PREFACE

MY excuse for writing this little book is that I have just returned from an archaeological tour through South Africa and Southern Rhodesia which I undertook at the kind invitation of the University of Cape Town, who besides generously helping towards the considerable expense of the trip had arranged for Mr Goodwin—formerly a pupil of mine and now one of the Senior Lecturers at the University—to accompany me. Critics may well enquire for whom exactly the book is intended. This problem has been a difficulty throughout. South Africans are becoming keenly interested in the early history of their country, and while the present work in no sense claims to give a complete account of it, I felt it a duty, both to the subject and to the University, to keep in mind the needs of the folk out there, many of whom are necessarily leading isolated lives, and have no access to current Prehistoric literature. On the other hand, it is important to bring to the notice of European prehistorians the very considerable amount of investigation that has already been done in South Africa; and this is all the more necessary in view of the close relationships which undoubtedly exist between the prehistoric problems of that far off land and those of our own continent. It has not always been easy to combine these two objects, and readers in one hemisphere must forgive me if, in the interests of those in the other hemisphere, they are sometimes bored. Those who already possess a general knowledge of European prehistory and the methods employed in its study might do well to skip lightly through the first two chapters. On the other hand, South Africans must look indulgently on the efforts which have been made to give some idea of their country with all its varied beauties to those who do not know it.

A certain amount of repetition too has been unavoidable as the same circumstances have to be examined from more than one point of view in different connections. In many cases

I have referred back to an account previously given, but this is such an exasperating proceeding that, where the matter is important and not too long, I have often thought it better to risk, to a certain extent, the charge of redundancy.

In no sense of the word does this book profess to give the whole story of South Africa's prehistoric past, and I have hardly dealt at all with the later phases, which come rather within the realm of the ethnologist. In the first place, although we covered some nine thousand miles or more on land, visited innumerable sites and studied a great many collections, we naturally were only able to cover a small part of the vast sub-continent. Further, the time is not yet ripe for a final authoritative work containing catalogues of all important sites, finds, etc. This will eventually have to be written, and it is a South African, or South Africans, who must do it.

It will be noted that little account has been given of skeletons. This is not because I have any desire to minimise the importance of such finds. It is rather because it seems to me that enough material has not yet been discovered to enable us to come to any sure or useful conclusions. The find at Boskop itself, although reinforced by somewhat similar discoveries elsewhere, cannot with certainty be correlated with an industry belonging to a definite culture, and I should hesitate personally to talk about "A New Species of Primitive Man"(7). There are those who go so far as to claim that Boskop Man is not really so very old. Again the exact significance of the human remains found at Broken Hill is still a matter of controversy. I feel, then, that it is safer, in the present state of our knowledge, for the prehistorian to continue unravelling the story on his own lines, though undoubtedly at some future time he will have to link up his results with those of the physical anthropologist when the latter has arrived at more certain conclusions. In this connection we await the appearance of an authoritative work by Professor Dart.

South African prehistorians are to be congratulated on what they have already accomplished, often in the face of considerable discouragement, and even ridicule. As in the case of all new countries, men's minds at first turn largely to the future and not to the past, with the result that any subject which cannot claim to provide immediately material benefits for the community is little encouraged. The now growing interest in their prehistoric archaeology, in their geology—apart from prospecting—and in other purely scientific investigations in South Africa is, in my opinion, a most hopeful sign indicative of national cultural development, indeed of the growth of a true South African nationality within the British Empire.

Everyone was so overwhelmingly hospitable and kind to us while we were in South Africa that the "Thank you" list is indeed a long one. I am especially grateful to the University of Cape Town, to Sir Carruthers and Lady Beattie, as well as to Professor Barnard and Mr Goodwin. Dr Gill, Director of the South African Museum, placed all the collections there at my disposal, and Miss Bleek and Colonel Hardy helped me to work at, and take notes of, their collections while at Cape Town. To Miss Wilman, Mr Power and Mr Cronin, who took us in hand while at Kimberley, giving up much of their valuable time to us, we are more than grateful, as also to Dr Maufe, Dr Ross, Mr Broderick and Mrs Taylor at Salisbury. Major Trevor came over especially to the Victoria Falls to discuss with us the problems of the archaeology there, and Colonel Carbutt motored us over almost impassable roads to visit distant painted sites of very great interest in the Fort Victoria district. Mr and Mrs Neville Jones were more than kind to us; we stayed with them several days near Bulawayo, and though far from well at the time, our host motored us many a mile to show us interesting sites. Professor and Mrs Hoernle's kindness to us on all possible occasions will never be forgotten, and Mr van Riet Lowe was indefatigable in showing us important sites and placing at our disposal all the results he had obtained after long and patient investigation throughout the Orange Free State. Prehistorians are awaiting a book from Mr van Riet Lowe! Dr van Hoepen of the Bloemfontein Museum, and Dr and Mrs Archer Isaac of Molteno, were very kind to us, as were the Reverend W. A. and Mrs Goodwin of Queenstown, who bore with us for more than a week and made it possible for us to investigate many sites in the district. Dr Bruce-Bays and Mr Jansen at East London, and Mr and Mrs Gladwin at Middledrift, were more than good to us as also was Mr Fitz-Simons at Port Elizabeth, and Mr Heese at Riversdale. At Grahamstown we were more than indebted to Mr Hewitt and Father Stapleton, who gave up most of their time to us while we were there, helping us to study the collections in the Museum and visit the sites in the neighbourhood. Finally, to all the other friends who were kind to us, helped our work or gave us hospitality or implements, we offer sincere and hearty thanks.

As regards the actual preparation of the book, my wife, who was with me throughout the tour, made the tracings of the art which are here reproduced as well as all the drawings of the implements, and she has also helped with constructive corrections in the text. In this connection too I have again to thank my aunt, Miss Parry, who has read through and corrected the proofs for Press, and Mrs Quiggin has kindly made the index for me. I am indebted to my father, Professor Burkitt, for the map facing page 1 which he has made to illustrate our work. The photographs are my own except the view of Makumbi on Plate I and the engraved giraffe on Plate VII which were taken by Mr Goodwin whose help throughout our tour was invaluable.

A small bibliography will be found at the end of the book. Numbers placed in small brackets in the text refer to it.

M. C. B.

Cambridge
1928

CONTENTS

ILLUSTRATIONS

1. Wellington.	5. Glengrey Falls.	9. Bambata.
Stellenbosch.	Tylden.	Nswatugi.
Villiersdorp.	6. Dordrecht.	10. Ematjeni river.
Hermanus.	Molteno.	
Fish Hoek.	7. Fauresmith.	11. Domboshawa.
Noord Hoek	Afvallingskop.	Makumbi.
2. Riversdale.	Klein Philippolis.	Beatrice Road.
Still Bay.	Brakfontein.	Quarry Site.
3. Glen Craig.	De Kiel Oost.	12. Zimbabwe.
Wilton.	Prospect Farm.	Gokomere.
Howieson's Poort.	Petrus.	Impey's Cave.
4. Middledrift.	Paardeberg.	Readman's Farm.
	8. Halfway House.	
	Pniel.	

CHAPTER I

INTRODUCTION

PREHISTORY deals with the story of humanity before the art of writing had been invented. We have, therefore, no contemporary records from those early bygone days giving us the ideas men had of their own history, nor any accounts of their customs, thoughts and feelings. It is difficult to define precisely the limits which bound the period covered by the prehistorian's researches. On the one hand they begin at that moment in Man's evolution when he emerges from the purely animal state. But as this evolution has been, in large measure, a mental process—we differ essentially from the higher animals in that we possess a more complicated brain—it is hardly possible to say definitely when we should consider that we have to deal with a real man or when only with some earlier, perhaps tool-making, forbear. On the other hand the later limit is also ill-defined and variable, for history obtained from written records begins at different times in different parts of the world. The Egyptians, for example, discovered the art of writing in very early times, so that their story for the last four or five thousand years comes within the scope of the historian proper, while many parts of northern Europe, which furnish no early documentary records, give the prehistorian a much longer period to work upon. Finally, in the case of South Africa this later limit is still more recent, for there is no written record of much practical use before the 17th century, and even then the accounts are both vague and, of course, fragmentary. It is just this fact that makes the study of prehistory in South Africa so interesting and important to the members of the various nationalities who have chosen to make that beautiful country their home, and who are in the process of forming a new South African nation within the British Empire. The present inhabitants have, often, very different origins; the one common factor in which all have a share and a concern is their country and its history. Prehistory with them carries the story of the land down almost to the day before yesterday, and that is just the reason why it is of peculiar interest to every intelligent South African, and it is in the hope of helping forward the study of the subject that I am trying here to give a general, but connected, account of the early prehistory of the country as I understand it and as it was unfolded to me in the course of a recent archaeological tour undertaken at the invitation of the University of Cape Town.

In perusing the book the reader will find that a number of words and expressions are necessarily used in a rather technical sense; it is therefore advisable to begin by giving proper definitions.

ARTEFACT

The word artefact is used to include all objects made or fashioned by prehistoric man. Such tools as scrapers, knife-blades, polishing stones, bored stones, weapons, awls, etc., are all artefacts; but so too are fragments of pottery and ostrich egg-shell beads, though the latter, together with other objects of decoration, may be more particularly classed as "ornaments."

INDUSTRY

An assemblage of artefacts at a given site, when all are of the same age, is the industry of the site. Should a locality have been inhabited at successive periods, there being in consequence more than one assemblage of artefacts belonging respectively to several different ages, then several different industries are said to occur at that particular place.

CULTURE

The word culture is very difficult to define. Naturally industries of the same age and made by the same people in widely separated districts are not identical, although many types of tool are common throughout. They will, however, have an evident connection, some common elements one with another.

To begin with, then, culture denotes an assemblage of industries made by people of the same stock. But besides this merely material explanation, something further is included that is in part denoted by the German word *Kultur*, something more abstract that gives us an idea of the way of life and mental outlook of the people we are dealing with. In describing a culture then, it is necessary to take into account, not only the various industries which occur, but also any other factor, such as art, burial customs, etc., which will help us to discover anything of the life and minds of the people.

CIVILISATION

The word civilisation will be rarely used. It denotes a larger unit than a culture. Thus we can talk of the hunter stage of civilisation as distinct from the stage when man became a grower of crops. Or again, when the domestication of animals was being practised, we may talk of a herdsman, or nomad, stage. Naturally a civilisation may, and often does, include several totally distinct cultures.

It is hoped that these definitions will enable the reader to understand such a description as the following which might occur on a label attached to a museum specimen: "A stone artefact of the Stellenbosch[1] industry, belonging to the Lower Palaeolithic culture of the Old Stone Age civilisation."

CULTURAL AND TIME SEQUENCES

It should be further understood that when a tool or an industry is compared with similar finds in another district or part of the world no connection between them is necessarily implied. Like conditions—climate, etc.—engender to a very large extent like requirements and as a result the production of similar types of tools. Is not the same necessity the mother of the same invention? When, however, two industries are said to belong to the same culture, a connection between the folk producing them is implied, although no contemporaneity in age

---

[1] The well-known University town 35 miles from Cape Town.

is denoted. It is a very important point, which should be clearly grasped, that when it is suggested that such and such industries in, we will say, South Africa belong to the same culture as other industries found in Great Britain, *no similarity in age is implied.* The industries in question in the one case may date back to only a few thousand years B.C. and in the other to 20 or 30 thousand years B.C. and yet the two sets of industries may belong to the same culture. Let us see how this may come about. Starting from a common centre or cradle, a people and their culture may have moved northwards and southwards simultaneously. After a time the culture of the northern trek, having served its purpose and come to an end, may have been replaced by something different, perhaps in the natural course of evolution, perhaps when overcome by an invading race with a new culture stronger or better adapted to the climate. In the case of the southward trek the migration may have been slower and of far longer duration owing to the physical conditions met with en route, but finally a congenial part of the world may have been found where it was possible to settle down undisturbed for many thousands of years. We may find then, at the end of the southern trek, a culture very similar to, though perhaps a little more developed than, its long vanished cousin of the north, but actually of far more recent date. So it cannot be too strongly urged that when industries in widely different parts of the world are correlated to the same culture, no implication of a similar age in time is intended.

The reader may have been wondering how, in the absence of written information, we discover any of the important facts or interesting details of prehistory. Obviously we can only study the objects these distant folk have left behind them on or in the ground and note how and where they occur. In this way we are enabled to piece together a certain amount of their story. In doing this, considerations of four kinds help us— Stratigraphy, Typology, Preservation and Patina, and Associa- ed Finds. These methods of attacking the problems will now be explained with special reference to their application in South Africa.

STRATIGRAPHY

The geological law of superposition states that when a series of strata occur one on the top of another the uppermost is the newest, and each successively deeper layer is older than the one which rests upon it, provided there has been no disturbance of the ground subsequent to the formation of the strata. If then the layers contain tools and ornaments we also necessarily arrive at a sequence of industries. This is, of course, only common sense. Suppose a number of people inhabited a room for many generations, bringing in dirt and rubbish which was never cleaned out, cooking their food on an open hearth in the middle and never clearing away the cinders, throwing aside their broken tools and the bones of the animals just eaten, while plaster fell unhindered from the ceiling and dust deposited itself from the air, thus adding to the general accumulation of rubbish, undoubtedly after a time the room would begin to silt up. People would no longer be able to get in by the doorway and the room would ultimately be filled with accumulated material almost to the level of the roof. If one of the walls were then taken down, a section would be exposed. The lowest stratum (i.e. the one on the floor) and all its contents would, according to the law of superposition, be of earlier age than the one covering it, and this, in turn, would be older than the next layer above, the most recent being the one next the ceiling. Thus the sequence of industries for the room in question could be determined; and if a number of such rooms were opened up, and the industries in them studied, we should be able to determine a sequence of cultures. This is exactly what the prehistorian does when he excavates some prehistoric home situated either in the mouth of a cave or under an overhanging rock.

Naturally not every "home" has been continuously inhabited throughout prehistoric times and, as a matter of fact, in South Africa, it is very seldom that on excavation we find more than one industry present. In Europe, where the climate, for long periods, made existence in the open uncomfortable, such sequences of industries and cultures are common, and combining all the information obtained from various excavations, the following table, giving the so-called Archaeological Record, has been compiled:

IRON AGE	CULTURES[1]
Late	
Early	

BRONZE AGE
Late
Middle
Early
Copper

STONE AGE
Neolithic or New Stone Age

Mesolithic or Transitional Age ... ...
{ Asturian, Campignian, Kitchen Midden, Maglemosean, Tardenoisean, Azilian }

Palaeolithic or Old Stone Age
Upper Palaeolithic { Magdalenian, Solutrean, Aurignacian[2] }
Middle Palaeolithic Mousterian
Lower Palaeolithic { Acheulean, Chellean, Prechellean }

Eolithic or Dawn of the Stone Age

It sometimes happened that a cave which had been used as a home remained for a period uninhabited, before it was re-occupied by people of the same or some other culture. During this untenanted period, an accumulation of earth and rubbish would take place naturally, but would of course contain no trace of man's handiwork. Thus a so-called sterile layer is

[1] Usually named after some type station where the culture was first discovered. For lack of space only the Palaeolithic and Mesolithic cultures are given.
[2] Often called Capsian in North Africa.

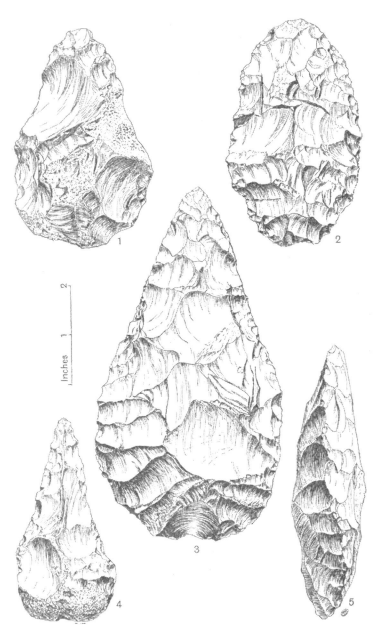

Fig. I. European Lower Palaeolithic *coups de poing*. 1. Chellean example from Stamford Hill, Middlesex. 2. Acheulean ovate from the Somme valley, France. 3. Pear-shaped Acheulean example from Hoxne, Suffolk. 4. Small pointed Acheulean example from Shrub Hill, Norfolk. 5. Acheulean ovate showing S-twist from the Somme valley, France.

formed. It is like a blank page in a printed book, and is often very useful to the investigator as it clearly separates the industries which occur above and below it.

In Europe the prehistorian has found it possible to subdivide still further the various cultures listed above. But these subdivisions are of local rather than universal importance, and with them we are not here concerned. South Africa is a long way from Europe and many of the corresponding cultures probably arrived at a rather later date, having in many cases undergone a slightly different evolution.

TYPOLOGY[1]

The typological method of approach to prehistory depends upon a careful study of the tools and ornaments themselves which we find in the prehistoric homes or in the open. These tools are by no means quite the same at all stages of man's development. Certain types of tool, it is true, occur over wide areas during a long period of time, but others only belong to certain definite cultures. It is evident that should an otherwise undated industry be excavated in which such a characteristic tool is found to be a prominent feature, it would be reasonable to assign it to that culture of which the tool is typical. However, on the strength of this evidence alone it would be unwise to dogmatise, unless the facts are further confirmed by stratigraphical or other considerations.

The different kinds of tools we find can readily be divided into families according to the various characteristics that they are found to present. Thus we have the family of the scrapers, implements which have the working edge sharp and usually very convex; of the awls, pointed tools for piercing purposes; of pointed knife-blades; of pigmy tools, etc.[2] It is sometimes possible to determine an evolutionary sequence in

[1] Figs. I and II illustrate the more characteristic types of tools found in European Palaeolithic industries.

[2] These families, in so far as they are found in Africa, will be described in the chapters on various cultures. Those who wish to go more deeply into the matter should consult some general work on Prehistory (5) (6) (44).

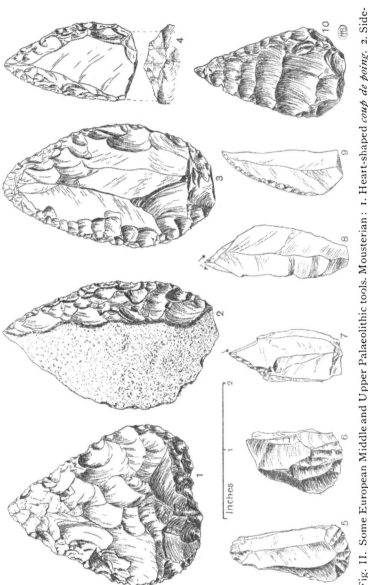

Fig. II. Some European Middle and Upper Palaeolithic tools. Mousterian: 1. Heart-shaped *coup de poing*. 2. Side-scraper. 3; 4. Points: note faceted striking platform. Upper Palaeolithic: 5. End-scraper. 6. Core-scraper. 7. Angle-burin; the burin facet is backed against a trimmed edge. 8. Ordinary burin; burin facet is backed against another burin facet. 9. Châtelperron point or knife-blade; the trimmed portion is really a blunting. 10. Solutrean laurel-leaf.

a family, showing how one tool develops from another, and this knowledge can be used by the prehistorian to obtain a chronological sequence of industries and so to check information derived from stratigraphical considerations. Obviously industries in which the original type of the tool occurs must be earlier in time than others in which a development of the type is found. Again, prehistoric man did not always employ the same technique in the manufacture of his tools. One such technique for trimming implements to which we shall have occasion to refer is known as "resolved flaking" or "step chipping." Instead of, as normally, directing the blow obliquely towards or at right angles to the edge of the implement to be trimmed, the blow is in this case directed inwards, more or less towards the heart of the material. The result is that the force of the blow only penetrates a short way into the stone, and the shattering action causes a fragment to break off which leaves a ridge or step where the original and new faces meet. (This technique is well exemplified in the Mousterian side-scraper, Fig. II, 2.) Sometimes, as we shall see later, the technique employed was determined by the nature of the materials used.

Stratigraphy and Typology are the two most important methods of study for the prehistorian. When working on cave or rock-shelter homes, the first has given us a sequence of cultures, and the second has analysed the industries which belong to these various cultures. The last two methods of study with which we now have to deal are essentially subsidiary. They are checks as it were which the prehistorian can employ locally to confirm the conclusions he has already arrived at.

PRESERVATION AND PATINA

Before the age of metal man made his tools of wood, bone, antler, horn and any other suitable material which he could obtain, but more especially of stone. Except in rare instances, or in the case of comparatively modern industries, wooden tools have not been preserved for us. But those made of the other materials enumerated, particularly of stone, are frequently

found. In the course of ages these various objects have undergone a considerable amount of weathering; in the case of sub-
stances such as bone, antler, etc., this has generally involved a
leaching out of the organic matter, and its replacement by
mineral material. When a bone still contains most of its organic
matter, in other words when soup could be made by boiling it
in water, then the investigator may be sure that the bone is of
no very great antiquity. Where, however, the organic matter
has been replaced by mineral material, there is no reason why
the object should not survive and be therefore of indefinitely
great antiquity. The weathering of stone implements may be
considered under two heads, (*a*) mechanical, (*b*) chemical. In
the first case the edges of the tool are more or less rounded and
blunted by being rolled about in a stream or by the sea, until
finally the original shape of the object may disappear and
nothing be left but a pebble. In the second case a chemical
change, usually involving an alteration in colour, takes place at
the surface of the object, penetrating to a greater or less depth according to the potency of the weathering agencies and the length
of exposure to them. This phenomenon is known as patination.

An interesting illustration of how the study of the preservation of an object can be used to check the results suggested
at first sight by stratigraphy is furnished by a cave above
Settle, in Yorkshire, called Victoria Hole. Here extensive
excavations were made away back in the eighteen-seventies,
and scrupulous care was taken in the digging. Every object
found was carefully labelled and marked on a plan to show its
exact situation in the excavation. Most of the infilling of the
cave consisted of glacial layers of great antiquity, but above
was a series of deposits containing artefacts belonging to the
Romano-British period, including a number of beautiful enamels.
It was disconcerting to the prehistorian of the day, and remained
so until recent times, that bones of the cave-bear (an animal
extinct long before historical times) were found associated with
the Romano-British enamels, and on the other hand that a
portion of bone which had clearly been cut with a metal tool
occurred in the bottom layer, stratigraphically below the glacial

layers mentioned above. As a matter of fact the actual situation was as follows. The bottom layer was not horizontal but was banked up against the back of the cave, and against this the later deposits were in turn banked up. The whole place had been riddled by rabbits and, in the process of burrowing, it had required no great effort on their part to shift the cave-bear bones more or less horizontally from the early into the later layers and to carry the cut bones from the top layer into the bottom one. In those early days of prehistoric investigation the destructive action of rabbits from the prehistorian's point of view was less realised, and but for the fact that the state of preservation of the cave-bear bones was totally different and far more mineralised than that of the fauna associated with the Romano-British enamels, while the cut bones found in the bottom layer were by no means deeply mineralised, it would not have been recognised that in the particular case in question the homely rabbit had completely nullified the conclusions drawn from stratigraphy—in other words that the "subsequent disturbance" mentioned in the law of superposition had actually taken place.

Another interesting example of the use of the preservation method to the prehistorian is the case of the De Kiel Oost surface site in the Orange Free State. Here an incredible number of implements was found covering half an acre or so of land near the Riet river. On examination it is at once evident that whereas the majority of the implements show little or no weathering, their edges being as sharp as when they were first made and there being no patina, or skin of weathered material, on them, in a number of instances the edges are more worn and the surfaces of the tools have become coated with a dull reddish-brown patina due to surface alteration. This fact alone would lead a prehistorian to suspect either that he was dealing with two distinct cultures, or with an earlier and a later industry belonging to the same culture. But if the tools are divided into a weathered and a non-weathered group it is found that though some types of tools occur exclusively in one group and not in the other, on the other hand a number of types occur throughout both groups. A combination of considerations of typology and preservation enable us, therefore, not only readily to distinguish an earlier industry from a later, but also to recognise both industries as belonging to the same culture.

ASSOCIATED FINDS

In studying an industry the associated finds must always be taken into account, as much useful information can be gained from them. As in the case of the preservation method just described, it is rather as a check on the information gained from stratigraphical and typological considerations that such observations are useful. By associated finds are meant all the other objects apart from artefacts that are found in the deposit, such as the bones of animals, whether of those eaten by prehistoric man or not. It is often possible to date the associated fauna from other considerations—geological or palaeontological—and for this reason the finding of bones is most important. The recent find of Lower Palaeolithic types of tools associated with mammoth teeth in the lower gravel terraces of the Vaal river, described by Professor Dart (10), will at once come into the student's mind. It is, of course, necessary in the first place to make sure that the associated finds are really contemporary with the industry in question, and in this connection considerations of preservation are useful. Take, for example, the case of the famous find of portions of a human skull at Piltdown in Sussex; the fauna occurring in the gravels included both earlier Tertiary species, these being very heavily rolled, and later Quaternary species, where the rolling and weathering was far less pronounced. The state of preservation of the skull itself corresponded with that of the Quaternary rather than with that of the Tertiary fauna. As a further instance of the use of a study of the associated finds, one may take the case of the tool, doubtless used as a javelin head and called a "laurel-leaf," which is made from a thin blade chipped over both faces till in shape it more or less resembles the leaf of a laurel bush. This type (Fig. 11, 10) is found in one culture (the Solutrean) of Upper Palaeolithic

times in Europe; but very much the same sort of tool is also
found in industries of much more recent date in Europe, and
throughout Africa at various periods. In Europe it is often important to be able to say definitely whether a given industry
containing laurel-leaves is really Upper Palaeolithic or not.
Where, however, the industry is found associated with the bones
of Quaternary fauna no doubt can exist, the associated finds
conclusively prove it to be Palaeolithic.

How far are these various methods for pursuing the study
of prehistory useful in South Africa? Theoretically, of course,
they are of universal application, but can they be applied to an
area like South Africa where the conditions, climatic and otherwise, are so different from those that we have to deal with in
Europe? Unfortunately, the stratigraphical method—the most
important of the four—has been, as yet, but little used. This
is due to various causes. In the first place, most of South
Africa is a very dry area of low rain-fall, and it is not, therefore, a region where deposits of soil rapidly accumulate. Again,
as in all dry areas, occasionally exceedingly heavy rains fall
and torrents are formed which sweep all before them, sometimes
carving out quite deep canyons in their courses. These canyons,
or dongas as they are called, may be as much as forty feet or
more in depth and only a few yards wide. Another year a
reverse process may take place, a new donga being opened
elsewhere, the donga of the year before being filled up with
silt. While the first donga was open, a near-by industry might
easily get washed in from the surface and then buried when
the canyon silted up. On subsequent excavation such an industry
would appear to have come from the immense depth of forty feet
under ground. No importance however could be attached to
this fact—there have been instances when lemonade bottles have
been unearthed from incredible depths! Lastly, to be perfectly
frank, South African archaeologists have not, as yet, paid enough
attention to the obtaining of stratigraphical evidence. This is
especially the case in such an area as Natal, which owing to its
higher rain-fall would seem to be especially favourably situated,
but where, from an archaeological point of view, the field is

almost entirely virgin, very little having as yet been done in the way of research or spade-work.

For the most part, too, such cave deposits as do exist are disappointing from a stratigraphical point of view, for it is rare to find a rock-shelter containing more than one industry. However, Mr Goodwin, of Capetown University, has excavated a cave at Montagu (Cape Province) with some success. Here an industry belonging to one culture was superimposed upon industries belonging to another and older culture (19). The position was somewhat similar at another cave near Fish Hoek (Cape Peninsula), where Mr Peers, the fortunate excavator, not only found a superposition of industries belonging to two cultures, but actually in both cases the skeletons of the folk themselves. It cannot be too strongly urged that far more attention should be paid in South Africa to this matter. Except where it has been demonstrated that only one industry is present, the practice of going out for an "afternoon's dig" in a local rock-shelter merely for collecting purposes should be replaced by a process of careful and scientific investigation—a process which is well within the compass of the amateur. If this is not done, much valuable information-giving data concerning prehistoric times in South Africa will be irretrievably lost.

The typological method, naturally, is as applicable to the South African industries as to our own; that is to say, families of tools can be determined and careful note can be made as to what types are found associated together in the different industries. Much good work has been done by South African archaeologists in this connection, and, as we shall see later, a number of distinct cultures have been determined. However, as has already been pointed out, it is always dangerous to rely exclusively on typological considerations.

The preservation method, as in Europe, is of importance in South Africa. One instance, that of De Kiel Oost (see p. 12) has already been given. In an area, however, where most of the industries are found on the surface, weathering, as might be expected, is rather capricious. Most of the industries found in the caves, judging from their little weathering, cannot be chronologically very ancient.

A study of the associated objects is often of great use. But in the case of surface finds it is often impossible to be quite certain that objects found associated with an industry are really contemporary. For example, it has been claimed by some that fragments of glass bottles, apparently chipped to form small tools, occur with Smithfield industries near the Modder river and elsewhere. If this were so, and if genuine glass tools made from bottles really occur contemporarily with a Smithfield industry, then the Smithfield culture must have been in existence until very recent times, indeed until after the introduction of the bottle a century or two ago.

Prehistorians in South Africa, for the most part, necessarily work locally, and, owing to the enormous distances which separate them from each other, have little opportunity of carefully studying the finds from other areas. The meetings of the South African Association for the Advancement of Science, however, act as important rallying points where the various local workers meet together to discuss their problems and describe their finds. As a result of a series of these meetings the following cultures and industries have been recognised as distinct from one another (16), (17)[1]:

Wilton ...   ... including   Kitchen Midden industries

Smithfield {Upper
           {Lower

Still Bay

Lower Palaeolithic including {Fauresmith
                             {Stellenbosch
                             {Pniel, or Vaal river } industries
                             {Victoria West

After a careful study of the problems I am inclined to make the following comments on this table. I suggest:

(a) That as the types of *coups de poing* commonly found in the Vaal river gravels do occur elsewhere in Stellenbosch industries it cannot be maintained that there was a separate Pniel, or Vaal river industry. As, however, these special

[1] In this connection prehistorians are particularly indebted to Mr Goodwin, who has been especially concerned in this work of coordination.

varieties are frequently found at Pniel and in the Vaal river gravels, it is convenient to regard them as Pniel, or Vaal river variants of a Stellenbosch type of *coup de poing*.

(*b*) That there was also at least the influence, if not the actual presence, of a Middle Palaeolithic culture, though so far no industries which bear witness to it have been found in a pure and unmixed condition[1].

(*c*) That undoubtedly Neoanthropic[2] man invaded the country long before certain Bushman tribes introduced the Wilton culture. This is clearly shown by the presence of typical Upper Palaeolithic burins at a site near Grahamstown, and a peculiar and more ancient industry in the lower levels of the Bambata cave (Matopos, Southern Rhodesia(1)). These industries belong to a different and earlier culture than either the Smithfield or the Wilton, and should surely appear in the table.

(*d*) That I, personally, would not be quite content to assign all the material from the Kitchen Middens, which are so frequently found along the south and west coasts of South Africa, wholly to the Wilton culture. The matter will be discussed more fully later, but I am inclined to class these Kitchen Midden industries as a separate culture; for the mode of living of the people who made them was fundamentally different from that of their contemporaries in the interior.

As regards the nomenclature of the various cultures, South African prehistorians are very loth indeed to accept the archaeological record as developed in Europe as the standard for South Africa. This is due to two causes. In the first place, the older prehistorians, such as Mr Johnson and others (31), (32), (40), took the European record as being absolute and forced the South African evidence to fit somehow or other into the European scheme of things. The result, of course, was a hopeless muddle.

[1] Mr Goodwin is in complete agreement with me on this matter but would like to call the culture after some locality where Middle Palaeolithic types of tools are commonly found. A good typical locality would be Glengrey Falls, near Queenstown, and the term Glengrey culture might be introduced.

[2] Professor Minns has suggested that properly speaking the word should be Neanthropic. As, however, the term Neoanthropic has found its way into literature, it is retained here.

As regards the major divisions, there does seem to be a certain amount of universality; but the smaller the subdivision, the more limited is its distribution. The second cause is the difficulty the interested general public seem to have in realising that no time correlation is involved when two cultures are connected together; that, for instance, when the Stellenbosch industry is assigned to the Lower Palaeolithic culture of South Africa, no contemporaneity with a similar industry belonging to a Lower Palaeolithic culture in Europe is implied. As a matter of fact, as might be expected in the case of an area like South Africa, which is so far removed from the cradle of the Lower Palaeolithic culture which was perhaps in North Africa, the two are probably actually widely separated in time.

The difficulty has been shelved by the use of purely regional names, and correlations with the more northern cultures have been tentatively suggested by but one or two investigators. From some points of view it is a good thing for South African prehistorians to work out the problems on wholly independent lines, so long as care is taken not to introduce terms such as "Old Stone Age" and "New Stone Age," giving them a significance different from that which they already have in Europe, a practice which would only cause confusion with the already existing European nomenclature. However, it does perhaps seem rather a pity not to correlate two cultures which are undoubtedly similar and were presumably made by people of the same stock, even if they are found many thousands of miles apart. This is all the more so as the intervening links between South Africa and Europe are being discovered by workers in other parts of the continent, such as Messrs Wayland in Uganda, Leakey in Kenya, Macrae in Northern Rhodesia, and others. The reader will find that in this book I have not hesitated to make the correlations which I believe to be justified. I should not of course go so far as to subdivide such major divisions as the Lower Palaeolithic, nor to attempt to distinguish in South Africa between Chellean and Acheulean industries, though as a matter of fact it will probably be found in the long run that this too is possible. In the present state of our knowledge, however, it would be doubtfully expedient.

CHAPTER II

GEOLOGY AND CHRONOLOGY

I N the first chapter we surveyed the scope of prehistory and
the methods employed for obtaining information, the question as to how far these methods are applicable to South
Africa and the results that have been obtained up to date. We
must turn our attention for a moment to another and a more
comprehensive record with which the prehistorian is concerned,
that is the story of the earth, and more particularly of South
Africa, as told to us by the geologist (12). Naturally, being on
such a big scale, this record is far less detailed than the story
of man as shown by the archaeological record. But it is important, for the archaeological record has to be duly assigned
to its right position in geological history. The archaeological
record has given us a sequence of cultures and information on
the industries and other activities of man at various periods,
but it has told us little of the environment and conditions,
climatic and otherwise, under which man had to live, nor anything about other contemporary life, nor of course does it
give any actual dates. The geological record therefore is very
important from our point of view, more especially as mankind is largely governed by climatic conditions. Again various
geological agencies have, in many instances, considerably altered
the face of the earth, even during the relatively short period
which has elapsed since mankind was evolved. Rivers have
been deepened, deposits have been laid down, and all such
changes have to be correlated with the archaeological record
which we have just discussed.

In Europe the matter has long been studied and has given
rise to much controversy. As might be expected, the geological
record is, itself, fragmentary, and the vastness of the whole
matter is almost appalling. Nevertheless, interesting correlations have been made. It often happens that tools belonging to

2-2

recognised cultures are found in datable river gravels. Perhaps open encampments of prehistoric people had formerly been pitched near the river where water and game might be readily procured. When in flood the river would overflow its banks and sweep away the tools and other objects dropped by man, which would be embedded in the sheets of mud and gravel which the river would deposit as it subsided again. When the archaeologist, maybe thousands of years later, finds these tools in an "unrolled" condition with the edges fairly sharp and fresh, he can claim that they have not been carried far from their place of origin or subsequently disturbed by water action or any other means, and therefore that they must date back to a period contemporary with the formation of the gravel in which they were found. Thus it is possible to assign a particular culture to the age of a particular gravel. Unfortunately, however, the geologist is not always able to date gravels and other Quaternary deposits accurately, and indeed he is all too prone to utilise the prehistoric tools he finds as fossils from which he may guess at the age of the strata containing them. A vicious circle results, the geologist using the prehistorian and the prehistorian making use of the geologist! Despite this, however, a great deal of work has been found possible in Europe, where the problem of dating deposits, although extremely difficult, is helped by the fact that during Palaeolithic times a large part of the Northern hemisphere was subjected to the alternate cold and warm periods of the so-called Great Ice Age. Students who wish to go further into this subject should read some work on general prehistory (5), (6), (44). It is sufficient to say here that throughout the Quaternary era, which coincides more or less with Palaeolithic times, there were several glacial epochs alternating with warm periods. During the glacial epochs actual ice sheets extended southwards over England, reaching nearly as far as the Thames. During the inter-glacial periods considerable ameliorations of climate took place, and at certain times the mean annual temperature may have been higher than it is to-day. The consequent alterations in the flora and fauna were, of course, great, and varied in extent at different periods. The study of the animal and vegetable remains which we find associated with various industries often enables us to assign cultures to definite periods in Quaternary times. Again a typical industry is sometimes found in stratigraphical relationship with a river terrace or a moraine formed during a definite glacial maximum (Fig. III). But climatic changes did not cease in Europe on the close of the Great Ice Age for, although there have not been any great changes in temperature, there have been considerable alternations of dry and humid periods. Again we can often obtain useful criteria enabling us, to a certain extent, to make correlations with definite geological periods.

Turning now to Africa, the problem appears in some ways much more difficult, and it is certainly far more obscure. Owing to its geographical position we cannot expect to find the same evidence for glacial and inter-glacial periods, even if the changes of temperature which so affected the northern areas ever took place in the latitudes of South Africa. Hardly any work has been done in this connection in Southern Africa. The few geologists living in the country are required to spend all their energies on commercial prospecting. One professor of geology told me pathetically that if he went out into the open country and stated that he was interested in its geology, he was thought to be mad, and in self-defence had to tell everybody that he was busy prospecting!

A visitor to the valleys of the Modder or the Vaal will at once notice that the sides of the valley do not slope down evenly to the river but form long steps or terraces (Fig. III). These terraces are composed of gravels and other material obviously laid down by river action. They are the remnants of gravel sheets formerly deposited over the whole floor of the valley. The fact that they occur high up above the present level of the river clearly indicates that at some past period the water must have flowed at a considerably higher level than it does to-day. In other words, the river has cut its bed down a good deal since the time when the upper terraces were deposited. The origin of such river terraces is interesting. Various causes operate to make a river capable of doing more work and of cutting down its bed to a new low level. One is a change in the slope of the ground due to earth movements or other phenomena, which thereby increase the velocity of the river. Another is an increase in the volume of the water. In the case of many of our waterways in England, we find that such an increase in the power of a river to deepen its bed is due to both causes. But in South Africa, where everything is on a very large scale and earth movements have for a long time played but little part, it seems probable that an increase in the volume of water has been the more potent factor. This increase may be the result of various climatic changes. In Europe the alternations of glacial and inter-glacial periods, the formation of glaciers and their subsequent melting, supply just such a cause. But it does not seem possible, at any rate at present, to postulate a similar state of affairs in the case of the gravel terraces of the Modder and other South African rivers; although the fact that four terraces exist along the sides of these river valleys and that we frequently find four such terraces in European valleys (Fig. III) is, perhaps, significant. Formerly it was suggested that these terraces were due to the ponding back of the river by hard belts of rock crossing the valley; in other words that they were shore lines of a series of lakes which fell rapidly to a new level when the barriers holding them up were finally broken through by the river. But if this were the true explanation, the terraces in question, fringing the river valleys, would be strictly horizontal and not sloped or "graded" as it is called with the valley bottom itself. In the short time I was in South Africa it was, of course, impossible to ascertain whether or not these terraces were graded to the present valley, but it would seem unlikely that they are truly horizontal. Horizontal lines occur so seldom in nature that they attract attention, even in a far smaller area of country than the section of the Lower Modder valley which we visited. Further, Dr Du Toit, the well-known geologist at Kimberley, who originally suggested the barrier explanation, told me himself that he had completely revised his opinion since finding, in the alluvial diamond diggings in the Lichtenberg

V = Present River Bed   T = Terrace   M = Moraine

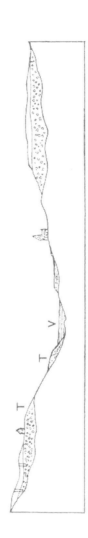

Terraces on the Vaal River near Windsorton (after Beck)

Fig. III. Diagrams showing the formation of river terraces in Europe and South Africa.

district, evidence for a stratigraphical sequence showing alternating dry and wet periods. This being the case, the subject of the terraces in the Vaal, Modder and Orange river valleys is one that should be examined *de novo* by some South African investigators without any further loss of time. The find of mammoth teeth by Mr Sheppar, near Bloemhof, Vaal river valley, published by Professor Dart (10), makes us hope that a few young geologists will be forthcoming sufficiently interested in the early history of their country to spend a little time away from the everlasting diamond, gold and other metal prospecting. For much valuable information could be gained which would help us to date South African industries.

In the case of the Vaal, the gravels of the top terrace indicate that at the period when the river laid them down it not only flowed at a far higher level than it now does, but that it also followed a rather different course. However, neither in this top terrace nor in the one below do we find any implements made by man. It is only in the two bottom, and therefore more recently formed, terraces that implements occur. Here the finds are exceedingly rich and the industries belong to the Lower Palaeolithic culture. A careful geological survey of all these terrace gravels would be specially welcome. In spite of the finding of mammoth teeth associated with these industries, I am inclined to consider that in South Africa they are rather more recent in time than the similar ones in the north. After all, proof has yet to be adduced that the mammoth in South Africa was contemporary with the same species in Europe. I would go so far as to suggest that there may be a difference of several thousand years between the age of South African cultures and that of their European counterparts. This would help to explain that definite feeling of greater modernity which the prehistorian experiences when examining the South African industries, and also the enormous quantity of implements that have survived. While in England we collect our finds painfully one by one, in South Africa they can be gathered up in sackfuls. Such is the prehistoric wealth of the country.

CHAPTER II

GEOLOGY AND CHRONOLOGY

I N the first chapter we surveyed the scope of prehistory and the methods employed for obtaining information, the question as to how far these methods are applicable to South Africa and the results that have been obtained up to date. We must turn our attention for a moment to another and a more comprehensive record with which the prehistorian is concerned, that is the story of the earth, and more particularly of South Africa, as told to us by the geologist (12). Naturally, being on such a big scale, this record is far less detailed than the story of man as shown by the archaeological record. But it is important, for the archaeological record has to be duly assigned to its right position in geological history. The archaeological record has given us a sequence of cultures and information on the industries and other activities of man at various periods, but it has told us little of the environment and conditions, climatic and otherwise, under which man had to live, nor anything about other contemporary life, nor of course does it give any actual dates. The geological record therefore is very important from our point of view, more especially as mankind is largely governed by climatic conditions. Again various geological agencies have, in many instances, considerably altered the face of the earth, even during the relatively short period which has elapsed since mankind was evolved. Rivers have been deepened, deposits have been laid down, and all such changes have to be correlated with the archaeological record which we have just discussed.

In Europe the matter has long been studied and has given rise to much controversy. As might be expected, the geological record is, itself, fragmentary, and the vastness of the whole matter is almost appalling. Nevertheless, interesting correlations have been made. It often happens that tools belonging to which is naturally tough as well as sharp, and secondary working along the edges of such tools as lance-heads, etc. is not only unnecessary but would be difficult to do neatly in the more refractory material. Fine-grained quartzites are often employed and sometimes even such coarse material as Table Mountain sandstone. Quartz, chalcedony and lydianite are frequently used for the manufacture of small tools, though for this purpose we very commonly find indurated shale, an almost slaty stone of fair hardness which occurs in many places as a result of dolerite intrusions into deposits of shale. This material is found commonly in the north-west part of the Cape Province and in the Orange Free State, and was much used by the people belonging to the so-called Smithfield culture whose most central settlements seem to have been in these districts. Indurated shale is not, however, confined to any one area and it was used throughout South Africa by prehistoric man.

A few words about the main scenic features of South Africa and Southern Rhodesia may not be out of place here before beginning a description of the more important archaeological sites we visited. From a geological point of view most of the sub-continent has been land for a very long period of time and the scenery as a whole has been largely determined by this long period during which the land has been exposed to atmospheric influences. No less than 40 per cent. of the area of the country, including Southern Rhodesia and Bechuanaland, lies above the 4000 feet contour line and we have to deal therefore with a high, dry and exhilarating climate. Sweeping down from the north there is a line of mountains, the Drakensberg range, which divides the comparatively narrow belt comprising Zululand, Natal and the native territory of the Transkei from the Transvaal and the Orange Free State. These mountains appear to be of no great height when viewed from the high plateau of the Orange Free State, but on the other side they fall steeply to the lower level of the eastern belt of country. Southwards the Drakensberg becomes lower and breaks up into a series of parallel ranges which, turning westwards, more or less follow the line of the south coast. They have various names: the Stormberg, the

Langeberg, the Outeniqua range and so on. This mountainous belt continues right along almost to the Atlantic. South of it the land is lower than in the interior and in fact forms a much broken-up coastal plain intersected by short rivers from the hills, many of which only flow in the winter. This mountain system has played a very important part in determining the climate of South Africa, for by thus cutting off most of the damp winds which blow from the Indian Ocean the interior plateau-land of the country is far drier than it would otherwise have been. Such is the dryness indeed that nowhere in the whole of the Union of South Africa is there a lake, or permanent sheet of water of any considerable size.

Geographically speaking, the Cape Province lies like a horse-shoe on the map, its western limb bounded by Bechuanaland and its eastern limb by the Transkei which lies just south of Natal. Embraced between these lie the plateau-lands of the Orange Free State in the south with the Transvaal to the north.

As in all dry lands, when rain does come it is in sudden deluges, and these rapidly carve out the dongas already referred to. The formation of these dongas or narrow canyons is a disturbing feature to the African farmer to-day, as a large quantity of valuable soil is thereby removed from the farms, and this is no light matter in a country where there is frequently no very great depth of soil.

The South African cultures already enumerated (see p. 16) have not all of them an even distribution throughout the country. The Lower Palaeolithic, it is true, occurs universally, but the various industries which are included in this culture are more restricted. The Victoria West industry is practically exclusively found in dolerite country, more especially in the Karroo. The Fauresmith industry is found mainly in the Orange Free State, but here the distribution seems to be rather wider than in the case of the Victoria West industry. The Still Bay culture was for the most part, as we shall attempt to show, a later, hybrid culture and is mainly found in the coastal areas south of the mountains. The more modern Smithfield and Wilton cultures, which were still in existence in the 16th century when Europeans first arrived in South Africa, have an interesting distribution The former is found mainly in the central parts of the country north and west of the mountains. The industries are principally made from the local indurated shale. Peoples belonging to this culture inhabited rock-shelters in the mountain ranges, especially on the slopes facing the interior of the country. Most of the rock engravings which we shall have to study, and many of the Bushman paintings found in the Union territory, were the work of Smithfield man. No Smithfield industries of any kind have been found farther north in the northern Transvaal nor in Rhodesia. The Wilton culture on the other hand is found chiefly south and east of the mountain system. Where it occurs in painted rock-shelters the art is quite different from that found associated with industries of the Smithfield culture. But the Wilton culture is also found in Southern Rhodesia and probably too in Uganda. It is very unfortunate that so little archaeological work has been attempted in Natal. It would be important to see how the Wilton, as well as perhaps still earlier, migrations of Neoanthropic man arrived in the south, and whether or no they followed an eastern route.

Finally a whole series of Kitchen Middens, many of them perhaps quite recent, but some older, are found fringing the sea-boards, especially on the west, south and south-east coasts.

CHAPTER III

SITES AND SCENERY

I MAKE no excuse for devoting a long chapter to a description of the archaeological tour through the Union of South
Africa and Southern Rhodesia which forms the basis of this
book. In the first place, so much archaeological work has already been done in South Africa as to make it impossible to
give a complete detailed account of the prehistory of the land
within the bounds of one volume, and therefore it is important
for the reader who is being introduced to the subject to know
exactly what will be the extent of ground covered. Secondly,
in subsequent chapters it will be necessary to utilise the evidence
which was obtained from work done at various sites, and it would
only distract attention and make the argument more difficult
to follow if at the same time there were given descriptions
of the sites themselves and information as to how they can
be reached. It is far easier if reference can be made back to a
previous chapter dealing with this side of the story. Finally,
"man is essentially a child of his environment," and it is
therefore important to give, as far as possible, a picture of
what his surroundings were. In view of the fact that until as
late as the 17th century of our era the history of South Africa
is, strictly speaking, prehistory, we may rightly assume that
during a long period of the story the conditions under which
man lived, climatic and otherwise, were more or less similar to
those obtaining to-day.

Starting our tour from Capetown, we took the train northwards as far as Hutchinson in the Karroo, whence a short
motor drive deposited us at Victoria West (Plate 1). This
small Karroo town is situated at the mouth of a narrow pass
through low hills or kopjes, the upper end of the gap being
closed by the wall of the dam which is optimistically expected
to secure the inhabitants' water supply. The Karroo country is

very characteristic, consisting of extensive plains, always more or less arid and especially so during periods of drought. At intervals these plains are cut into by dykes of dolerite forming low, flat-topped, wall-like ranges of hills, which, when more broken up, become amazingly regular conical kopjes. They are all covered with screes composed of dolerite boulders, which through age-long weathering action have become patinated a dull sandy-red colour. There is a sense of space in the Karroo, but the dolerite dykes prevent that depression usually engendered by vast plains and an unbroken horizon. The few localities where a good and constant water supply occurs must have been almost ideal from prehistoric man's point of view, for game abounded on the plains.

A little to the west of the town has been found the Victoria West industry, about which controversy has raged. This industry will be described in due course. Tools belonging to it can be picked up from the surface of the ground at the bottom of one of the little kopjes, and excavation has shown that similar tools can be collected from at least 15 feet underground. However, depth means very little when we are dealing with the bottom of a scree-covered hillside where the boulders composing the scree may be presumed to be continually sliding down towards the bottom of the valley.

About 200 yards or so to the west of the town, and about 10 feet above and to the left of the path leading to the dam at the base of the kopje "Moonlight Hill," a Smithfield site occurs.

The industry is mostly made of a hard black indurated shale which is found on the hillside opposite, across the valley. It includes small end-scrapers, small cores, awls, quantities of irregular flakes and fragments of ostrich egg shell. The area in which it is found is very restricted. The site is a purely surface one resting on a sort of limy tufa.

From Victoria West we motored 60 miles or so over the Karroo towards the little township of Vosberg, actually stopping at Keurfontein, a farmhouse about two miles east of the place. During this drive we were able to appreciate something of the reluctant fascination which this semi-desert country

PLATE I

Victoria West and the karroo country beyond.

View of granite country near Makumbi, S. Rhodesia.

has for those who know it well. Imagine a single track—by courtesy called a road—pursuing its way relentlessly, for there are no turnings off or byways, over miles and miles of reddish, sandy, dusty veldt, never going much uphill, never going much downhill, skirting round the base of each succeeding kopje. No grass, no bushes, but a low greyish scrub speckling the dry soil all over and providing a meagre living for flocks of thirsty sheep. The track is narrow—there is no question of traffic, you meet perhaps one car and a few donkey wagons—you pass some half-dozen lonely farms each with its water-wheel and a square of scraggy, optimistically planted trees. But at evening all is changed, incredibly softened, and the kopjes, glowing red and gold with sunset colours, cast amazing purple shadows.

But to return to Keurfontein; a mile or so south of the farmhouse is an isolated kopje with a flat top. Some of the rocks forming the scree on its sides are of great size, being many cubic yards in dimension, and they have weathered to a black or dark brown colour. They also occur strewn over the flat top which is about a quarter of an acre in extent. It is just as if some mighty force had pelted the top of the hill with gigantic cannon-balls and grapeshot. In the middle is an immense boulder undercut by weathering on one side, thus forming a sort of natural rock-shelter. This must have been used by prehistoric man as a shade from the sun just as it was used by us in 1927. All the ground around is littered with Smithfield tools comprising the usual end-scrapers, awls, fragments of ostrich egg shell, flakes, and the like. A large number of the boulders themselves, especially those on the top of the kopje, have been engraved, and, as will be seen in a subsequent chapter, it was found possible to distinguish a chronological sequence in this art, there being several styles and techniques present. From the top of the hill a very good view was obtained; in the direction of Vosberg itself, and beyond the farm Keurfontein, the ground appeared to be lower; probably at some period, when the climate was slightly damper than that of to-day, the whole region was vlei or fen. It struck me on the spot that this prominent kopje covered with engravings may have formed a central rallying place for the numerous peoples who would have found good hunting around these vleis.

If this were so, one might perhaps suggest that the engravings were not simply due to the *joie de vivre* of a single family or tribe living on the hill-top, but were connected with the fact that it was a central meeting place, or may perhaps even have had a ritual significance. The fact that a chronological sequence of the engravings could be obtained demonstrated that the site must have been utilised by prehistoric man for a long period. Vosberg seems to be very typical of its kind, and it is interesting to note that later on, when we visited other and similar sites farther east in the Orange Free State, similar engravings were found and a similar chronological sequence was recognisable.

After examining the Vosberg site we continued northwards towards Kimberley, famous for its diamonds and its dust. Some little distance before reaching this town the railway crosses the combined Modder and Reit rivers which join together a few hundred yards above the railway-bridge. Below the railway-bridge, a quarter of a mile from the left bank of the river and resting on a gravel terrace, there is a very interesting late Smithfield site. Tools are found over a wide area and become exceedingly numerous as the centre of the settlement is reached. Scrapers, awls, and other typical Smithfield tools made from a greyish-greenish indurated shale occur, and also a number of chipped fragments of bottle glass which may or may not be contemporary with the Smithfield industry itself. The site was admirably suited for prehistoric habitation. In front lies the river, providing a constant supply of fresh water, while the banks are fringed with trees affording an agreeable shade. Behind, at some distance, is a second gravel terrace, and behind that again a low range of hills which help to temper the winds blowing over the plains. The ground itself is dry and powdery and of course the whole area is very dusty; but except for this inconvenience it must have been an ideal spot, food being plentiful and water always present.

From Kimberley an important excursion was made to Pniel on the Vaal river, one of the most interesting sites we were enabled to visit. On our way we stopped at a low kopje, now called Halfway House, on the left-hand side of the road where formerly there had been a Bushman village. Many of the boulders had been collected and arranged to form hut circles, in one of which Mr J. Power, of Kimberley, had, some time previously, found a small flint arrow-head, tanged and winged, a type of tool of which only four or five examples are known in South Africa.

The kopje is very isolated and conspicuous and, as at Vosberg, a large number of rock engravings occur. Time did not permit a detailed study of these, but we were unable to find any examples similar to the earliest series found at Vosberg (p. 146), all having been made by a technique and in a style that our investigations at Vosberg had shown us to be fairly late.

The sites at Pniel itself lie close to the now disused German Mission Station. In the gravels of the Vaal river, especially where they have been dredged up by the diamond seekers, any quantity of Lower Palaeolithic *coups de poing* are to be found. They are made from a local greenish-grey coloured rock, and include the well-known Pniel variant types which will be described later.

An investigator coming from Europe is especially struck by the extraordinary wealth of archaeological material. It was impossible to bring away even a tithe of what we saw, and it was extremely difficult to make a satisfactory choice so as to produce a representative collection and not merely one composed of *chefs d'œuvre*; one literally scrambled over heaps composed of little else than *coups de poing*.

On the ground above flood level, between the river and the Mission Station, a late Smithfield industry composed of the usual tools was found, and on the top of the kopje behind the Mission Station a number of rock engravings were studied. These however showed no example of the earliest style and technique.

Alexandersfontein Pan, near Kimberley, is a particularly

interesting site. There is a sort of vlei about 4 miles from the town and close to the popular resort, Alexandersfontein. For countless ages industries left by prehistoric man on the surface of the ground around have been washed into this vlei and to-day in dry seasons these are found in any quantity at this spot. It is easy to recognise that older elements are present as well as more modern Smithfield tools, etc. What would certainly seem to be a strong Middle Palaeolithic influence can be observed in the technique of many of the tools.

From Kimberley we went straight to Salisbury in Southern Rhodesia, where we found ourselves in a completely different kind of country (Plate I). The local rock was often granite, irregular kopjes and hills, frequently formed of one enormous rocky dome, rose out of the surrounding bush and rather rank grass. We passed large areas of cultivated country, more frequent streams and more trees which afforded a welcome shade from the now tropical sun. Here our attention was largely engaged in studying the "Bushman" paintings of the district, which were so important that the scientific results will be found in a separate chapter. Some sites occur close around Salisbury itself, but the two most important (Domboshawa and Makumbi) are some 20 or 30 miles north of the town within the borders of the Native Reserve.

From Salisbury we went to the Victoria Falls, where we had the advantage of discussing the local archaeology and geology with Major Trevor of Livingstone. There seems to be very little question but that Professor Lamplugh was correct in his explanation of the archaeological sites at the Falls (36). The implements found there are treacle-coloured and are made of the chalcedony which is found at the base of the Kalahari Sands and is of Tertiary age. The tools are on the surface of the ground or under thin wisps of river gravel resting on the basalt bed of the old valley of the Zambesi, fringing the edge of the present magnificent gorge. They have been thus found for some 10 miles below the present Falls, and it is argued that at the time when they were fashioned the Falls must have been about 10 miles further down stream than they now are, and that the people who made the implements lived in settlements on the banks of the river which flowed peacefully just below them, not having yet fallen foaming into the gorge. At first sight it does seem incredible that the 10 miles of immense gorge could have been carved back subsequent to mankind's existence in these regions, but, as Dr Du Toit pointed out to me, the basalt is not homogeneous, there being two lines of weakness corresponding to the directions of the zigzags of the present gorge. Water working along these lines of weakness would cut back the rock very quickly when once it started to do so, perhaps at an average rate of a yard or two a year; it is probable, however, that there was no great change for a long time and then a more or less sudden recession to a new lip. That the thin wisps of gravel in which the implements occur have been laid down by tributary systems such as the Maramba river, which flows into the Zambesi from the north some distance above the Falls, is a well-nigh impossible suggestion when the local circumstances are taken into account. Further, it would appear that the particular variety of chalcedony from which the tools are made is not particularly common in the valley of the Maramba itself, while on the other hand the material from which tools in that valley are made does not seem to occur on the sides of the gorge below the Falls. The industries in question belong to the Lower Palaeolithic culture; typical *coups de poing* occur together with flakes, trimmed all over the top and showing occasionally a faceted prepared platform. From a typological point of view, the existence of a faceted prepared platform perhaps argues for the existence of a Middle Palaeolithic influence. The evidence afforded by these sites around the Victoria Falls suggests a considerable antiquity for the Middle and Lower Palaeolithic culture in this northern portion of South Africa.

Returning to Bulawayo, we visited an interesting stretch of country which we were told is typical of many others where Lower Palaeolithic industries occur. This is about the Ematjeni river, in the month of July a dried-up watercourse in the Esipongweni district some 19 miles from Bulawayo to the left-hand side of the Lonely Mine Road and a little short of Harman's store.

The undulating veldt of this district is sparsely covered by bushy growths—for the most part of a prickly nature. On following the river bed until its junction with the Kokwe river some few miles below, a number of *coups de poing* were collected, many showing the peculiar technique of the Vaal river or Pniel variants (p. 66). Naturally the specimens were for the most part rolled, especially when found near the middle of the river bed. Many of the rivers in Southern Rhodesia have yielded these Lower Palaeolithic industries, more especially those flowing northwards from the watershed which lies to the south of the Zambesi. For example, very good specimens were seen in Mr Neville Jones's collection from the Inyati and Embuzini rivers and similar ones have been found in the bed of the Shangani river in the Lebakwe and Charter districts, as well as at the famous site at Sawmills on the Umgusa river, where not only do *coups de poing* occur but also industries which seem to show a strong Middle Palaeolithic influence.

While at Bulawayo we had also an opportunity of visiting a number of Bushman painted caves in the Matopo Hills, and here we were enabled to confirm the information obtained from the evidence of the painted sites near Salisbury. Not only did we study the Pomongwe and other Bushman caves regularly visited by tourists on their way to the "World's View," but also, thanks to Mr Neville Jones, we examined the Nswatugi Cave, 3 miles from Whitewater—15 miles or more as the crow flies beyond the "World's View" itself.

Thence we passed on to Fort Victoria which is situated in a district interesting not only on account of the Zimbawe ruins some 17 miles away, which will be described separately, but also because of the existence thereabouts of a large number of painted rock-shelters. These include the famous one described by Dr Impey (Plate II), which lies on the farm "Iram" just off the road to 'Ndanga and some 40 miles from Fort Victoria itself. Besides painted rock-shelters, there were a number of interesting sites near Fort Victoria containing implements. Especially important is the excavation being undertaken by Father Gardner of the Jesuit Mission at Gokomere some 11 miles north-west of

PLATE II

Near and distant views of "Impey's Cave" near Fort Victoria, S. Rhodesia.

Fort Victoria. The site in question lies close to the Mission Station in a rock-shelter not far from water, in undulating and park-like surroundings. A typical Wilton industry has been discovered comprising all the well-known pigmy forms, mostly made from clear quartz. When one remembers what a difficult substance this is to chip, it is amazing to find these thousands of tiny tools so skilfully manufactured. Towards the base of the excavation two tools made from shale were discovered, which, if found in Europe, would probably be assigned, on typological grounds, to a Middle Palaeolithic culture and described as Mousterian points[1].

Father Gardner has also discovered *coups de poing* at the side of a vlei near by, one of which, made from quartz rock and about 5 ins. long, is of extreme beauty and skilful manufacture. The Fort Victoria district as a whole must in many ways have been a paradise for prehistoric man, except that owing to its situation only 3500 feet above sea level there must formerly have been as great a tendency for the inhabitants to become fever stricken as would be the case to-day were the uses of quinine unknown. With this exception the country is perfect, being park-like and fairly wooded. The ground is undulating, with low ranges of hills, many of them of granite, which give to the hill-sides those broad round features so characteristic of much of Southern Rhodesia.

From Fort Victoria we took the train to Johannesburg, stopping *en route* at the small junction of Gwelo. Gwelo lies in a plain at the base of a large wooded kopje at the bottom of which a number of *coups de poing* are to be found. In winter a small stream flows through the plain; in its banks and on the dry bottom were found tools which certainly belong to a later culture than the Lower Palaeolithic and show in their technique a Middle Palaeolithic tendency. The fact that the *coups de poing* occur in a terrace (?) deposit at a considerably higher level than

---

[1] Father Gardner has since informed me that a hollowed stone mortar similar to those found in other Wilton industries has been found near the bottom of the excavations. These would appear, therefore, to belong to the Wilton culture throughout.

these tools would seem to indicate that we have here a veritable stratigraphy, the industry showing Middle Palaeolithic tendencies being clearly the later, as it occurs at a lower level in connection with the present river system. It was not possible, however, in the time available to work this out in greater detail. It is a locality where it might be worth while to do some further investigation.

Visiting Pretoria the collections in the museum were examined, and here we saw an example of the evil effects of not having a sufficiently numerous expert staff in a museum. A good deal of very valuable archaeological material is coming into the museum from the alluvial diamond diggings of the Lichtenberg district and elsewhere. Some of this material is extraordinarily interesting and would probably yield exceedingly valuable information which would help to correlate the various industries with the geological record of the country if careful investigation were undertaken. It is not too much to say that it is quite likely that the whole branch of the subject dealing with the correlations of the various cultures in South Africa with the geological record, could be elucidated if a young geologist, keen on the Quaternary period, were on the spot. Such is not the case, however, and precious evidence is being allowed to be lost, while there is nobody with the necessary time and expert knowledge even to label and describe the specimens which are sent to the museum.

From Pretoria we went to Bloemfontein, whence—thanks to the very great kindness of Mr Van Reit Lowe—we visited, in the course of a long circular motor tour, a large number of Fauresmith and Smithfield sites as well as rock engravings which occur in the western part of the Orange Free State. We left Bloemfontein by the Jagersfontein Road and passed over a rather arid region, very like what we had seen in the Karroo, but good sheep-farming country. The road rises imperceptibly to a low watershed and then descends to the valley of the Riet. Just before we reached the low causeway over the river we stopped to visit a site near the right bank on the left-hand side of the road. It is named Klein Philippolis, after the farm on which it is situated. The site covers about an acre of ground and contains any number of flint implements. They are all on the surface and include end-scrapers of every variety, awls, trimming stones, etc.; pottery and bored stones have also been found. The industry belongs to the Smithfield culture. The site must have been very convenient for prehistoric man, situated as it is just above flood level but close to water and with abundant game on the surrounding veldt. On the opposite side of the river several other sites have been discovered. In fact, all this area close to the Riet river is little more than one immense Smithfield settlement. On typological grounds one would assign the industry of Klein Philippolis to an Upper Smithfield culture, though one or two rather older tools may perhaps belong to a Lower Smithfield stage.

Leaving the Riet for a time we passed on towards Jagersfontein, crossing the Process Spruit *en route*. At the water's edge, close to the bridge, several much-rolled implements were collected consisting for the most part of large rough flakes made from indurated shale. It was difficult to assign them to any definite culture, but I believe we have here, as so often in South Africa, an example of a Lower Palaeolithic industry showing strong Middle Palaeolithic influences.

From Jagersfontein we reached Fauresmith, passing by Prospect Farm where further examples of these rather indeterminate industries were collected. The river bed near Fauresmith is simply full of Lower Palaeolithic tools belonging for the most part to the Fauresmith industry. The richness of this country in *coups de poing* is simply astounding. While most of the specimens we saw were lying in the river bed, having been washed out in the course of floods, some were collected *in situ* from the gravels of the river bank itself. The country around Fauresmith is rather more undulating than that near Bloemfontein and the town itself is dominated by low ridges of hills. The river runs right through the little town and implements can be collected literally at one's back door.

Leaving Fauresmith next day, we came to Brakfontein, a farm some 15 miles away on the Koffiefontein Road. Here we examined two very interesting sites. That on the right of the road down by a little stream yielded a rich Smithfield industry, consisting of a number of Lower Smithfield tools. On the left of the road an ancient sand dune had been cut through by a donga, exposing the ground below and washing out a number of implements in the process; this site yielded a Fauresmith industry. Some soft limy marl had also been deposited here in which Fauresmith *coups de poing* occurred. As usual, both sites were pleasantly situated and a constant water supply could always be obtained from the little stream just mentioned which runs down to join the Riet river some miles below. The general view was very characteristic of those parts of the Free State which are not great plains, but which consist of shallow valleys dominated by boulder-strewn dolerite kopjes and hills. Passing through Koffiefontein, we stopped to examine the first of two tall isolated kopjes on the right-hand side of the road to Jacobsdal. This kopje is known as Afvallingskop, because many of the rocks seem to have rolled down its side. Many of the boulders strewn over the flat top have been engraved as at Vosberg; and it was interesting to note that the chronology determined by the super-positions of styles and technique there held good, with certain modifications and additions, at Afvallingskop. The scene from the top of the kopje was glorious. Once again the country was flat except on the horizon, where the usual dolerite hills were visible, the red colour of the patinated boulders forming as it were a dull framework to the scene. Below, a mile or so away, flowed the Riet river, giving a constant water supply and the picture was delightfully completed by the little village of Koffiefontein, with its broad streets and its wide-verandahed houses nestling below.

Continuing our journey, we were about to cross the Riet river at De Kiel Oost, but just before reaching the bridge we visited, on the left-hand side of the road, what is perhaps one of the most interesting Smithfield sites in the whole of South Africa. As at Klein Philippolis the settlement, which occupies about half an acre of ground, occurs above normal flood level. The richness of this De Kiel Oost site in all kinds of Smithfield tools is indescribable. Among other objects we had the rare good fortune to alight on a small piece of rock, engraved with a simple geometric pattern (Fig. XVIII, 1). We also discovered a small crescent made from chalcedony, the first of its kind to be discovered in the Orange Free State in a Smithfield industry (Fig. XVII, 15). It had a distinctly Wilton-like appearance, and its occurrence at De Kiel Oost supplies further evidence to show that the Wilton and the Smithfield were contemporary cultures though for the most part predominating in different geographical areas. Since I visited the site I hear that Mr Neville Jones has discovered another crescent, showing that the one we picked up was not a mere chance find, but that there is a definite intermingling of the different cultures. Especially at the lower end of the site, i.e. the part furthest from the road, there are obviously two distinct kinds of patination present. In the first case the black or dark greenish-coloured indurated shale from which the tools are made is hardly patinated at all; in the second case the surfaces were covered with a brown skin of patina of some considerable depth. On dividing the artefacts according to patina it was found that certain definite types of tools only occurred in the second, much patinated, series. It has been argued that we have in all probability to deal here with an older and a later series in the Smithfield culture which have been called the Lower and Upper Smithfield respectively.

We slept that night at Jacobsdal, a typical, if somewhat bare Free State "dorp," and next day crossed over a low watershed to the Modder river, when we had an example of the sudden changes in general outlook that are possible in South Africa. During the night it had rained and in the morning the whole scene was completely altered; all the hard outlines of the distant hills had become smoothed off, and instead of the characteristic broad dusty plain of the Free State we were in a country which, except for its wide extent, strongly recalled parts of Scotland. Incidentally, this country can be very treacherous for modern travelling after a slight rainfall. It was impossible to move straight forward in the car even with the help of chains; the shallow surface soil of the veldt, including that of the road track, had the consistency of boracic ointment!

However, this would not have affected prehistoric man to any very great extent.

Reaching the Modder we turned back towards Bloemfontein, passing a small Smithfield site on the way. It is interesting to note that whereas the Smithfield folk were numerous in the Riet river valley, their settlements are a good deal rarer in that of the Modder river. Why this should be so is difficult to say. The districts must have equally abounded in game, and the Modder—although, as its name implies, often muddy—would equally furnish a constant water supply.

It was not until we came to Paardeberg that we met with an important factory site; this is above the Modder on the left-hand side of the road, and on the left bank of the river. Here we found numerous flakes and trimming stones and lumps of raw indurated shale; very few finished tools, however, were collected.

Passing through Petrus we visited a Fauresmith and Smithfield settlement close to a spring which wells up beyond the village, on the left-hand side of the road. Having conveniently "punctured" just by the site we had ample time to examine it! That night we slept again at Bloemfontein, having had an extraordinarily interesting and illuminating three days' tour in the Free State. The general impression given by the Smithfield culture in this region is one of modernity. While the Lower Smithfield of De Kiel Oost, Brakfontein and elsewhere may date somewhat further back, the general impression gained by the investigator on the spot is that the Upper Smithfield, at any rate, continued to be a lively culture until at most a few hundred years ago.

Before leaving Bloemfontein for the south we made an excursion eastwards to see the painted rock-shelter at Modderpoort. The country here is quite different, being mountainous; indeed, we could see the Maluti range which joins the Drakensbergs. The hills round about Modderpoort are composed of what is known as cave sandstone, from the fact that it weathers unevenly, forming numerous rock-shelters. The surface of the sandstone is fairly even and very suitable for the paintings. Later, further along the railway line towards Durban, we visited similar paintings at Van Reenan, a village on the top of the famous pass over the

Drakensberg range, from which there is a wondrous view
stretching over the lower lands of Natal as far as the horizon.
On the commonage there we found, too, a nice little industry
though rather indeterminate as to culture. In the painted cave
itself diligent search yielded us nothing at all in the way of
artefacts.

Molteno and Dordrecht, both farming towns of a certain size,
were our next centres, whence we made excursions to various
sites in the neighbourhood where paintings are to be found.
This is classic country for the type of Bushman paintings which
were so admirably reproduced by Miss Helen Tongue in her
book (48). Aliwal North and Herschel, where the late Mr Stow
so enthusiastically studied and traced examples of this art (47)
back in the sixties and seventies, were not far off; and it was
important to compare the art of this region on the one hand
with that found further north at Modderpoort and beyond again
in Southern Rhodesia and, on the other hand, with that which we
were to see later to the south and east of the mountain chains.
At each painted rock-shelter implements were collected and
these were invariably found to belong to the Upper Smithfield
culture, all varieties of the ubiquitous end-scraper or "duck bill,"
as it is called in South Africa, being present as well as the
usual trimming stones, etc. Judging from our experience at
De Kiel Oost, tools typical of Lower Smithfield times were
completely absent, leading one to conclude that the Bushman
art of this region is not very ancient in time, perhaps indeed it
is only a few hundred years old. The fact, too, that considerable changes and deterioration seem to have affected the
paintings, even since they were examined by Mr Stow, also
gives the impression that the art is fairly recent in date. I am
not now referring to the hideous vandalism practised by picnic
parties in South Africa (the natives do not touch these places),
whose favourite pursuit, when not flinging stones at the painted
animals, is to outline them roughly in white blackboard chalk,
a material very difficult to get rid of and which completely
ruins both the appearance of the paintings and their availability
for serious study.

The aspect of the countryside is totally different hereabouts from that of the Free State. The region is far more hilly and Dordrecht itself stands over 5000 feet above sea level in the broken country close to Basutoland. The hills are high and steep and are often composed of sandstone similar to that at Modderpoort, but in between them there is a wide undulating upland, very suitable for sheep farms to-day and doubtless equally pleasant country for primitive man to inhabit in the past. A sufficiency of water exists and, unlike the Karroo, serious droughts are of comparatively rare occurrence.

Queenstown, a large, clean, pleasant town, is a very good centre for the prehistorian, as from it any number of interesting sites both painted and otherwise can readily be reached.

Though not so high as Dordrecht, the country is still very hilly and we are not yet wholly east of the mountain ranges. The broad valleys wind among the hills and the whole refreshingly green district is well watered by the Black Kei and its tributaries. Our kind hosts, the Rev. W. A. and Mrs. Goodwin, enabled us to investigate numerous painted rock-shelters both close to Queenstown (Rockwood, Ella's Farm) and further afield (Tarkastad, Tylden, etc. (Plate VI)). At most of these sites implements were collected which, as near Dordrecht and Molteno, all belonged to a late Smithfield culture.

Smithfield industries were by no means only found at painted sites, but also at several open-air settlements which we examined. One interesting spot close to the left bank of the little stream on the right-hand side of the road going up to the dam, just before a bridge is crossed, yielded a number of Smithfield tools of extreme freshness and without any patina, in spite of the probability that the settlement itself was somewhere a little higher up the stream, and that the implements we found had been washed down and redeposited in the soft earthy material on the river bank. Nevertheless, if this be so the settlement must have been close at hand as there is no trace on the tools of any rolling action. It was really inconceivable that these tools could be of any great antiquity. If they had been they must surely have either been rolled or patinated to some extent.

The two most interesting settlement sites, however, were at

PLATE III

The prehistoric site near the Glengrey Falls.

The "vlei" near Fish Hoek where a Still Bay industry occurs. Colonel Hardy is in the foreground and directly above him Mr Peer's cave can be seen.

some little distance from Queenstown. One was at the mouth
of the little gorge which is cut through the basalt below the
Glengrey Falls to the left of the road from Queenstown to
Lady Frere, and just in Kaffraria, i.e. native territory. The site
(Plate III) is on the left bank of the stream above normal flood
level and at the base of a low kopje. The tools are for the most
part patinated, some deeply, and the types collected showed
strong Middle Palaeolithic affinities with possibly some Neoanthropic influence. Implements showing resolved flaking up
both sides and a faceted platform, which in Europe would be
unhesitatingly accepted as Mousterian points, occur (Fig. XI).
Besides these implements we collected some heavily patinated
discs. On the other hand, rough core scrapers, small chopping
tools and the like were also found which suggest connections
with some later culture. This Glengrey Falls site seems to be
one of the best for demonstrating the presence in South Africa
of a strong Middle Palaeolithic influence.

At the second site (Bouwers drift), which is situated on either
side of the road from Queenstown to Tylden just before it crosses
the Black Kei, exactly the same state of affairs occurs, but in
this case either we missed the actual centre of the settlement
or it was not so rich in material.

From Queenstown we passed by East London to Middledrift,
another area of especial importance to the prehistorian. The
tiny village of Middledrift lies on the railway from East London
to Port Elizabeth, but though it stands 1600 feet above sea level
it is definitely to the south-east of the mountain massif. Though
some Smithfield tools were discovered many Wilton examples
were also found. But Middledrift was more especially interesting
on account of the Lower Palaeolithic industries found there.
These not only occur scattered over the commonage, but also
under gravel beds deposited by the river when it flowed at
a considerably higher level than it does to-day. Very fine
examples, too, have been found a mile or so west of the
hotel at a depth of 15 feet in beds exposed by a deep donga,
known as the Euphorbia donga on account of the large number
of *Euphorbia* trees near by. The catchment area near this donga

is very small and the hillside above quite low. That material to a depth of 15 feet has covered the deposits containing implements argues for a considerable antiquity for this industry, which is Lower Palaeolithic in culture, as evidenced by the large number of *coups de poing* found therein. The donga itself need not necessarily be of any great antiquity, even a small catchment basin will yield enough water during periods of deluge to form a rushing torrent which will rapidly cut down many feet through the soft material. The significant fact is the great depth of material deposited all over the area on what would seem to have been the surface of the ground in Lower Palaeolithic times. Besides *coups de poing*—which, as I have said, are found not only *in situ* deep down underground but also washed out over the commonage—there are a number of clearly defined types of tools difficult to assign with certainty to any culture. For example, rough balls of quartzite chipped all over occur as well as pyramidal objects made from the same material showing fluted sides and more or less flat bases (Fig. VII, 5). There are also what might quite reasonably be called Mousterian points.

From Middledrift we passed on to Grahamstown, and here we found ourselves in the lovely green belt of south coast country between the mountains and the sea. It was likewise pure Wilton country. Whether we were examining the painted rock-shelters in a krantz of the Botha river to the left of the road to King Williamstown and 6 miles from Grahamstown, or whether we were excavating at Wilton (Plate VI) itself, nothing but regular and typical Wilton industries were found. The Bushman paintings were quite different from those we had previously examined and which had been associated with the Upper Smithfield culture. Instead of well-drawn figures, often in several colours, we had poorly-drawn animals and conventionalised men in bright red on a smudgy red background. Human hands, too, were often figured. Wilton itself is, of course, of especial interest as being the type station for this culture. The rock-shelter opens in a narrow gorge some 35 miles from Grahamstown on the way to Alicedale and some

7 miles or so from the latter place. It is actually on the farm Wilton, and is 2 miles from the homestead itself on the Alicedale side. The rock-shelter is long but not very deep, and the whole surface of the back wall is covered with paintings. The ground is dry and powdery and contains a large quantity of wood ash—by no means a pleasant material to shake through a sieve on a hot day with very little wind! As is almost always the case in South Africa, only one industry occurs; that is to say, the rock-shelter has only been inhabited by folk belonging to one culture. Implements were found, however, at a good depth and it is reasonable to suppose that the occupation covered a considerable length of time. We found the usual small round scrapers, awls, ostrich egg-shell beads and so on which are typical of the Wilton culture and which will be described in due course.

But perhaps the most interesting site near Grahamstown was a small rock-shelter difficult of access in the middle of a krantz which dominates the valley at Howieson's Poort. Leaving the hotel at the bottom of the Poort, one crosses the stream and strikes out so as to reach the top of the rocky krantz which faces one. Then, with the help of a rope attached to what appears to be none too secure a tree, one lowers oneself down with much trepidation to the rock-shelter lying some 30 feet below. The site was only discovered a few years ago by the children of the innkeeper, who succeeded with monkey-like skill in reaching the rock-shelter from below. The whole site is almost concealed by bushes and vegetation. The excavation was undertaken by Mr Hewitt, Curator of the Albany Museum at Grahamstown, and Father Stapleton, Rector of St Aidan's College, who found an industry which is certainly not Wilton but comprises numerous large flakes, discs, long rough crescent-like implements, some objects like those found in Still Bay industries, and above all eight typical burins (p. 81 and Fig. XIII). These latter are the first of their kind to be recognised in the Union, although one, or possibly two, had been discovered previously by Mr Neville Jones in Southern Rhodesia. The Howieson's Poort burins belong to various types—ordinary burins, angle burins and single-blow burins being represented. This shows that the possibility that the burin facet was unintentional and only made by chance is untenable. If found in Europe these artefacts would unhesitatingly be classed as Upper Palaeolithic. The importance of this find will be dealt with in due course. So far they are unique of their kind, but in all probability further research will bring to light other examples. Many local investigators in South Africa have never had the opportunity of seeing burins and may therefore sometimes have failed to recognise them in their finds, in just the same way as a medical man in Europe may have read about some tropical disease but quite naturally fails to recognise the complaint when he meets with it for the first time.

The Grahamstown area is exceedingly rich in prehistoric sites and as yet not a tithe of them have been investigated. We may expect important results to accrue from a careful study of this area, situated as it is south-eastward of the mountain massif, and enjoying totally different conditions, in respect to climate, etc., from the districts of the plateau lands on the inland side of the mountains which we had previously visited. Although at the time of our visit even this coastal region was suffering from drought, in more normal years the eastern part of the Cape Province, situated close to the sea, has a far more equable climate than the regions of the interior.

Next, thanks to the kindness of Mr FitzSimons, we visited a number of Kitchen Midden sites which fringe the coast for some 20 miles or so south of Port Elizabeth. It is usual for South African prehistorians to class all these Kitchen Middens as belonging to the Wilton culture, and many people in Europe call them "Strandlooper" sites. My impression is that neither description is really quite correct. "Strandlooping" rather than "Strandlooper" would seem to be the more correct expression, and it is quite possible that many different peoples at different times took to this mode of life requiring the manufacture of a number of specialised, but essentially simple tools, which because they were required were naturally soon invented and manufactured. But this again will be more particularly elaborated in a subsequent chapter.

Unfortunately time did not permit a visit to Mr FitzSimons' excavations in caves in the Zitzikama district where Kitchen Midden industries have been found apparently superposed on older industries, and a large number of skeletons have been unearthed.

From Port Elizabeth we went to Durban by boat to see something of the finds in Natal, but here we were grievously disappointed from an archaeological point of view. No serious work has been done, and yet this is an area of considerable rainfall and aggradation where important stratigraphical sequences might be expected and much evidence obtained.

Returning to Port Elizabeth, we made our way to Mossel Bay, where the hillside above the town yielded numerous *coups de poing* of Lower Palaeolithic date as well as much Kitchen Midden material. Mossel Bay is an inlet of the sea on the south coast. The town of the same name is built on the steep hillside not far from the point which is known as Cape St Blaize. The view obtained from the high ground above the town over the bay and towards the Outeniqua range of hills beyond is of surpassing beauty. In the foreground is the sea and then 10 miles or so of a coastal plain rising up to a considerable height; it is very irregular and much broken up by valleys; behind all stands the jagged outline of the mountains, cutting the hard blue sky. At just the same view must Lower Palaeolithic man have looked out, for the best sites we found were in sandy country covered with many varieties of flowering protea bushes just close by the golf links whence this glorious prospect could be seen. In all probability the *coups de poing* found on the surface have been washed out of the sand and are not absolutely *in situ*. I suspect that if excavations were carried out here these tools would be found to occur at some little depth: but the present surface of the sand is, of course, always shifting. With them are found Kitchen Midden flakes and implements, but these probably belong to a purely surface industry, and under any circumstances their appearance is far fresher than that of the yellow, weathered, quartzite *coups de poing*. The best hunting ground for Kitchen Midden industries, however, was close down on the bay at the seashore, where several sites have been observed. Kitchen Midden folk also lived in a large cave below the lighthouse at the end of Cape St Blaize. Similar cave sites have also been noted further round the coast. As is usual with these settlements, the inhabitants seem to have largely subsisted on shell-fish, for there are immense heaps to be seen, composed of the empty shells.

From Mossel Bay we travelled by the so-called "Garden Route" as far as Riversdale. For long stretches the edges of the railway-line are carpeted with brightly coloured mesembry-anthemum flowers of brilliant purple, gold, or pink. Riversdale is a convenient centre for those who wish to visit Still Bay— the type station for the culture of this name. It lies at the mouth of the Kafferkuils river some 23 miles from Riversdale. We had an opportunity of visiting the sites there in company with Mr Heese who was the first to investigate the district. Industries belonging to Lower Palaeolithic, Still Bay, Wilton and Kitchen Midden cultures are all found hereabouts. The Wilton industries, however, seem to be mainly confined to a number of definite sites mostly occurring in an intermediate belt between the Still Bay and the Kitchen Midden sites, the latter being close to the present seashore. The true Still Bay industry seems to be confined to the side of a limy ridge, to-day largely covered with blown sand, which can be traced from a point close to the river diagonally across country to the sea to the right of the estuary. It is possible that all the area seawards of this limy ridge—an area which now forms a sort of cape composed of sand dunes stretching out on the right bank of the river—was formed after the end of Still Bay times and that the limy ridge itself was once the margin of the coast. Should this be the case we have a ready explanation for the relative position of the industries belonging to the various cultures. In Wilton times the land stretched out beyond the limy ridge, but not as far as when the Kitchen Midden folk inhabited the district. We should expect, then, to find the Kitchen Midden sites fairly pure, an admixture of Kitchen Midden with Wilton industries on the Wilton sites, and a mixture of all the three industries on the limy ridge. And this is exactly what happens. The true Still Bay industry, however, is readily recognised by its peculiar state of preservation which differentiates it easily from either the Wilton or the Kitchen Midden industries. The Wilton sites themselves contain an immense quantity of small crescents, scrapers, awls and the like and yield a rich harvest to the collector.

On the other side of Riversdale, some 7 miles away from the town and high up in a krantz on the right bank of a small stream to the right of the road to Ladismith, is a painted site known as "The Cave of the Hands" (Plate VII). The large airy rock-shelter is much concealed by trees and bushes. Excavation has yielded a rich and typical Wilton industry, and the paintings recall exactly those of the Botha river (Grahamstown) and of Wilton itself. They belong to the style that we learnt to associate with the Wilton culture. Innumerable representations of very small human hands occur. Only one industry is found in the rock-shelter; therefore, alas, no evidence of any sequence of cultures can be obtained from stratigraphical considerations.

Mr Heese was formerly at Britstown in the Karroo country, where he made a rich collection, mainly of Smithfield tools. Both Upper and Lower Smithfield types occur there, the former including a large number of very beautiful specimens. One object in his collection interested me exceedingly; it was a heavily patinated artefact made of indurated shale which recalled strongly the tanged Mousterian points found in North Africa probably belonging to the Mousterian culture. Although the notches determining the tang were comparatively simple affairs, this tool should in all probability be correlated with the similar specimens of the north.

From Riversdale we returned to Capetown, having completed a tour of between 8000 and 9000 miles in the course of which we met with unvarying kindness and hospitality. At Capetown we spent some time visiting the sites in the vicinity. The industries found in the Cape Peninsula are of special importance. By the time the various migrations of cultures had reached this southern extremity of the continent, some hybridisation had already taken place and, owing to the fact that no further southward movement was possible, still further developments of mixed cultures took place in this region. This was especially the case with the Still Bay and Wilton cultures, and as a result the industries belonging to them are here more developed and mature in appearance than those further north and east. There is an important site not far from Fish Hoek, an outlying suburb of Capetown on False Bay. At this point the massif of the Cape Peninsula is broken through, there being low ground right across from ocean to ocean. Apparently the southern part of the Peninsula was originally an island, the intervening channel being now silted up mainly by sea sand. Projecting out into this low country there is a spur running down towards Fish Hoek from the more northerly mountain massif. On the top of this spur there opens a large rock-shelter which is in process of being excavated by Mr Peers and his son (Plate III). Rich collections have been made and two different industries determined.

In the upper 6 feet of material only Kitchen Midden tools were found but with them were discovered several Bushman skeletons. Below there were 9 feet or more of deposits containing industries which on typological grounds would be assigned to the Still Bay culture, and with them was discovered a skull totally unlike and far heavier and more massive in appearance than the Bushman heads excavated from the upper Kitchen Midden layers. This skull awaits description, and it will be very important to learn whether it is to be allied either with the Boskop find or with the type of skull found by Mr Leakey at Elementeita in Kenya. This is the first time that any human remains have been discovered associated with a Still Bay industry, and indeed it is the first time—unless we are to suppose that the industry at Howieson's Poort is also Still Bay in culture but with a stronger Neoanthropic influence— that a Still Bay industry has been found in a rock-shelter and in stratigraphical sequence with another industry.

On the main road from Fish Hoek to Noord Hoek at the bottom of the hillside at the top of which opens Mr Peers' rock-shelter, is a small "vlei" which is concealed by bushes and wattle from the view of the passer-by (Plate III). Here also a large number of Still Bay tools have been collected, many examples being of peculiar beauty. Unlike those from the cave, they are sand polished and have a peculiar putty-coloured waxy appearance.

Further along, and nearer Noord Hoek, the ground falls and the whole area consists of a sandy waste interspersed with vleis, sometimes full of brackish water. The sea is kept back from covering this area by a line of sand dunes a mile or two to the west. As is the case nearer Fish Hoek, a large number of beautiful Still Bay implements have been discovered on these sands and, as might be expected, they are exactly similar in appearance to those from the former locality. At one particular spot along the western edge of the first vlei reached by the traveller *en route* from Fish Hoek to Noord Hoek, and to the left of the road, there is a very rich Wilton site that has yielded numerous and beautifully made characteristic tools.

Thirty-five miles north of Capetown lies the small University town of Stellenbosch. This is an important place from the point of view of South African prehistory and it has given its name to the characteristic *coup de poing* industry belonging to the Lower Palaeolithic culture. The tools are yellow in colour and are made from a quartzite material which has been roughly and boldly chipped into the required shape. While most of the *coups de poing* are collected on the surface of the ground around Stellenbosch, we had the pleasure of discovering several examples 2 feet underground in what appeared to be brick earth. The exact site is a shallow quarry to the left of the Capetown road just after crossing a small stream close to the main railway-station. *Coups de poing* sticking into the ground and clearly *in situ* can be collected from the sides of the quarry. We were unable in the short time at our disposal to investigate this very interesting site thoroughly. It is possible that further research would unearth the remains of an associated mammalian fauna; it might also be possible to find shells of mollusca which might give an indication of the climatic conditions prevailing at the time.

Further northwards, near Wellington, we were also able to collect *coups de poing in situ* in a deposit formed of disintegrated Table Mountain sandstone, but here it is unlikely that anything of a bony nature would have survived. The implements found were of the usual "Stellenbosch" type.

The "Stellenbosch" industry is of fairly common occurrence around Capetown in the vicinity of the hills bordering the northern margin of the Cape Flats. Further eastwards specimens have been discovered near Villiersdorp—in two cases over a foot in length—and we ourselves found the industry near the village of Hermanus, on the neck of ground joining the prominent little kopje which dominates the village and the hillside beyond. In the kopje itself there is quite an interesting little cave where excavation has yielded Kitchen Midden material associated with crescents, etc., and therefore to be assigned more particularly to the Wilton culture.

Having now described the more important sites that we visited, the next few chapters will be devoted to discussions in greater detail of the various cultures and industries.

CHAPTER IV

THE LOWER PALAEOLITHIC CULTURE

IMPLEMENTS belonging to the Lower Palaeolithic culture are found very commonly in South Africa and in Southern Rhodesia. As indicated in Chapter I, a number of different groups of industries have been recognised; for the most part these are purely of regional importance, and it has not yet been possible to determine with any certainty a chronological sequence among them. Together they make up the Lower Palaeolithic culture of South Africa and are named, after the various localities where the particular tools typical of the industries are especially predominant, the Victoria West industries: the Stellenbosch industries, with which are included the Pniel or Vaal river type of implements, classed by some prehistorians as a separate industry group but here treated as a variant within the Stellenbosch group: and, finally, the Fauresmith industries.

THE VICTORIA WEST INDUSTRIES (Fig. IV)

These industries present several interesting and difficult problems to the investigator. Examples of the various tool types were first recognised some years ago by Mr Jansen at what has become the type site in the talus at the bottom of the hillside close to the little town of Victoria West in the Karroo. Tools have been discovered down to a depth of 15 feet, but this circumstance is probably of no great importance as the depth is doubtless due to accumulation of talus—a process which does not necessarily involve any great lapse of time. The material from which the tools are made is almost always dolerite, and it is to this fact that I personally would attribute the peculiar form and technique of many of them. The industry is assigned to the Lower Palaeolithic culture on the ground that ordinary *coups de poing*—not always made from dolerite—

have been found associated with the special types. The state of preservation of the various implements is not always identical, but the patina is deep and the tools are often much weathered, and, considering the nature of the rock, are in all probability of considerable antiquity.

Two distinct types of tool have been recognised: one beak-shaped (Fig. IV, 3), the other at first sight not unlike a somewhat flattened horse's hoof in shape (Fig. IV, 2). The chief feature of the tools is the almost invariable occurrence of a great flake scar on the under surface, showing a deep negative bulb of percussion. This is caused by a blow struck along the under margin of the tool. The under surface at the butt end is boldly trimmed, two, three or more flakes being removed, their edges intersecting the main flake scar just mentioned. In the case of the beak-shaped tools the upper surface is also boldly flaked and there is a distinct keel ending in the point. As a rule this keel does not run along the whole length of the tool; there is often a flat, natural surface left, more or less parallel to the flake scar below. The general appearance of the tool is not unlike a rostro-carinate. In the case of the hoof-like tool, the flaking on the upper surface continues all round, forming a rough, very flattened sort of cone. Owing probably to the nature of the dolerite material itself the tools are large, bold and heavy, and, in their present state of preservation, the edges are far from sharp. In colour they are a dull, sandy red.

The *coups de poing* found associated with them are of a normal kind and well made considering that good flint material was not available for their manufacture. One example (Fig. IV, 1) is made from a fine-grained quartzite, is deeply patinated, and in shape exactly recalls the industry belonging to the Lower Palaeolithic culture found in the bottom terrace of the Vaal river. Besides these tools a certain number of rough discs and chopping tools have been noted.

If the dolerite boulders forming the scree on the hillsides around Victoria West be examined, many of them will be found to have been fractured by ordinary natural means. There results, as a rule, the removal of just such a great curved flake

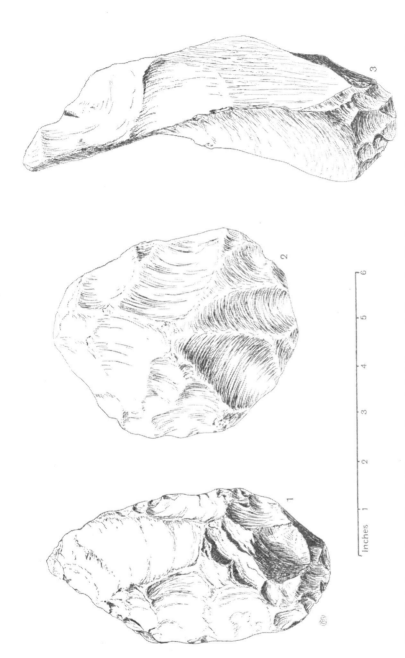

Fig. IV. Industry from Victoria West. 1. A *coup de poing*. 2. A "horse hoof"; the under portion consists almost entirely of a flake surface. 3. A beaked tool showing flake under-surface and typical under-trimming.

inches 1 2 3 4 5 6

as is seen on the under surfaces of the type tools. The boldly trimmed edge at the butt end, however, is of course absent on the naturally fractured examples. Therefore, apart from the trimming on the upper surface, this fact alone differentiates the tools from the natural specimens.

That the peculiarities of the tools can be connected with the nature of the material seems to be further shown by the general distribution of the industries, as, for practical purposes, they are only found in areas where dolerite occurs. Thus on a boulder-strewn kopje called "Halfway House," near Kimberley (p. 33), we came across an excellent example of the hoof-like type among the dolerite boulders. This probably indicates that the site had been occupied by Lower Palaeolithic man, and that the material to hand being dolerite the industry was of the Victoria West type. Another example was found on the hillside above the village of Fauresmith, in which district Fauresmith tools made from indurated shale and fine-grained quartzite lie scattered all around. Here again the probable explanation of the occurrence is that doleritic material was to hand.

The opinion held by some prehistorians that all the typical Victoria West finds have been naturally fractured seems difficult to maintain. It appears to my mind more probable that prehistoric man noticed that the available dolerite fractured readily in this particular manner and, making use of the knowledge, copied it artificially. To suggest a use for the hoof-like tools is a hard problem, unless they may be considered as a peculiar form of disc, and therefore as a sort of heavy chopping tool. The beaked implements would clearly be useful for many purposes.

Mr Goodwin has suggested that none of these objects were used as tools but that they were "tortoise cores"; in other words that prehistoric man's primary concern was to remove the flake from the under surface, and that this flake was then trimmed all round to a sharp edge and used in the same way as the well-known Levallois flakes so commonly found in early Mousterian industries in Europe. This may have been true in the case of some of the gigantic specimens now preserved in the Bloemfontein Museum by Dr Van Hoepen. It is strange, however, that if Levallois flakes showing secondary working round the edge had existed they should not be often found. Again, in a normal-sized specimen, the flake taken off would, after suitable trimming, have become very, very small. In the case of one perfect little example of a beaked tool now in the museum at Bloemfontein, strongly recalling in form the rostro-carinate, it would have been almost microscopic.

THE STELLENBOSCH INDUSTRIES (Figs. v–ix)

Tools belonging to a Stellenbosch industry were among the first to be recognised as prehistoric artefacts in South Africa and were forwarded to London for examination as long ago as 1866. As the *coups de poing* closely resembled those found shortly before by M. Boucher de Perthes in the Somme Valley gravels and accepted by Messrs Prestwich and Evans as definite artefacts made by Quaternary man, they were taken as belonging to the same culture. This correlation still holds good, although we now distinguish more clearly between cultural and time sequences and the acceptance of a connection in culture does not imply in any way a contemporaneity in age.

The Stellenbosch industries have a wide distribution throughout the Union as well as Southern Rhodesia. Naturally the material from which the tools are made varies to a certain extent in different areas, and the final appearance of the implement also varies slightly with the different materials. In spite of this, however, there is a remarkable uniformity in shape. The most usual material used is fine-grained quartzite, often sand-coloured. Two localities where very typical industries occur are Stellenbosch itself and Mossel Bay, a south coast seaport described in the last chapter, where hundreds of tools can be collected on or near the surface of the sandy dunes bordering the golf links.

The typical tool is the ordinary pear-shaped *coup de poing* (Fig. v, 2 and Fig. ix, 5). It is boldly flaked all over, the butt end being sometimes sharp, sometimes blunt. In the latter case some of the original smooth crust of the large pebble, from which the tool was made, has frequently been allowed to remain. Usually

not much secondary working along the edge can be seen, but this
could not be expected in such refractory material as quartzite,
and though not often straight the edges are wonderfully sharp
and even. The pear-shaped variety often shows slight variations
in shape. For example, there is sometimes a cutting away of
one side towards the butt end, producing a sort of shoulder; in
one or two instances this takes place on both sides, producing
a double-shouldered object forming, as it were, an immense
coarse tang (45). In all probability, however, these tools, which
are rarely found, were merely attempts to attain better hand
grips. *Coups de poing* are occasionally found in which the pointed
end is not in line with the central lengthwise line of the tools,
but lies outside it to the right or left (Fig. IX, 4).

South African *coups de poing* vary considerably in size.
I have seen some only a few inches long and others at least
a foot in length. For example, there are two measuring 12
inches in length from Villiersdorp (Fig. VI) that, even if used
as two-handed tools, would be very clumsy and heavy to work
with. It is difficult to imagine how these immense implements
could have been used. The more normal-sized examples, however, were doubtless employed in the same way as similar tools
found in North Africa and Europe. As the late M. Cartailhac
used to say, they must be considered as stone hands serviceable for any purpose for which the real hand of flesh and
bone would be too soft and would get too much cut about and
damaged. Thus, should digging be required, the pointed end
could be vigorously driven into the ground; should bone
smashing be the object, one of the sharp edges would be quite
suitable for the purpose; even if it were a question of breaking
somebody's head with a blow, these tools would still be quite
efficient weapons for performing the operation[1]!

The S-shaped twist corresponding to that so often found
in Europe in Acheulean times (Fig. I, 5 and Fig. IX, 3), is often
to be noted. This is seen when one holds the implement
sideways with one edge nearest to the eye; it is then clear that

---

[1] It is of course quite possible that some of the smaller ones may have
been hafted at the end of a split stick, or by some other means.

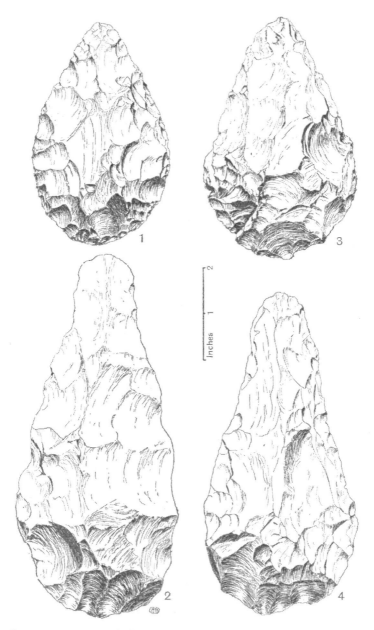

Fig. V. Lower Palaeolithic tools. 1, 2. Stellenbosch *coups de poing* from Pniel, Vaal river, and Villiersdorp, C.P. 3, 4. Similar tools for comparison from Ouahila and Tabelbala, both sites in Southern Algeria.

the line of the edge, instead of being more or less straight, forms an elongated **S**-shaped curve[1] just as if the top half of the tool had been rotated slightly upon the bottom half. Why this **S**-shaped twist occurs and whether or not it was made on purpose is completely unknown. Some writers have suggested that a gyroscopic motion would be induced when such a twisted *coup de poing* was thrown, and that this would ensure success in aiming. If it were a question of throwing by hand this could hardly be the case—consider the relatively feeble force of a hand throw compared with the weight of even a small stone. But it would be interesting for someone skilled in sling throwing to experiment and see whether a surer aim could be attained when using twisted tools. In Europe the **S**-shaped twist does not occur before Acheulean times.

In Europe, too, besides the pointed pear-shaped *coup de poing* of Acheulean times, similar though finer than its Chellean forbear, there also occurs an oval development known as the "ovate" (Fig. I, 2). As a rule this tool is considerably flatter than the pear-shaped variety and, as its name implies, is oval in shape. Also whereas the older tool was fairly symmetrical about a central lengthwise line, the ovate is often symmetrical about a central crosswise line as well. Generally the edges all round are sharp, although one is usually blunter than the other, and a small flat platform can sometimes be detected on this edge, indicating that these tools were probably held in the hand, the blunter side being against the palm. They would then form quite efficient chopping tools. Ovates (Fig. V, 1) are of frequent occurrence in South Africa and are often beautifully made in spite of the refractory materials available. As in Europe they vary much in size from a few inches in length to nearly a foot; these latter tools must have made quite formidable choppers. The **S**-shaped twist down the sides, described above in connection with the pear-shaped variety, also appears among ovates both in Europe and in South Africa (Fig. IX, 3).

Normal *coups de poing* or ovates were sometimes made from large flakes, but they were chipped all over, so that little of the

[1] The curve is often that of an inverted **S**, i.e. Ƨ.

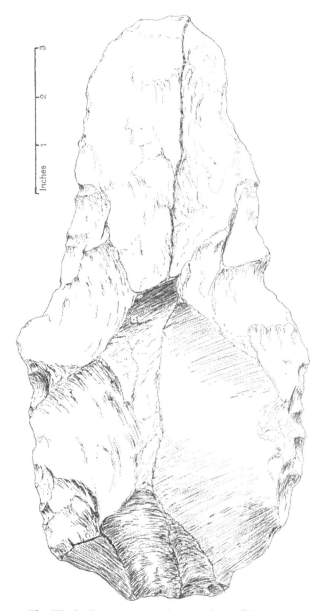

Fig. VI. Stellenbosch *coup de poing* from Villiersdorp, C.P.

flake surfaces remained, both faces being covered with relatively small flake scars. In most cases, however, they were core tools, i.e. tools which were made by taking a block of material and chipping it into shape, the flakes being thrown away.

Besides *coups de poing* a number of untrimmed flakes occur, as well as some rough scraping tools showing a certain amount of coarse trimming along the working edge. There are also disc-like tools varying in size, though the average diameter is not large. They are boldly and not unattractively chipped so that the flake scars run from the circumference towards the centre of the object at which point it is of a certain thickness, thus giving the disc a somewhat diamond-shaped cross-section through its centre at right angles to the plane of the circumference. Sometimes, however, the object is more nearly spherical and the flake-scars run in all directions. These tools may possibly have been used as large sling stones (Fig. VII, 1). In this connection may be mentioned the finding of a large number of round stone balls which vary considerably in size. At first sight these balls might be thought to be natural, but similar ones have been found in large quantities by Mr Macrae in the middle levels of a cave at Mumbwa in Northern Rhodesia, where they are associated with a late Lower Palaeolithic industry, showing perhaps Middle Palaeolithic tendencies (37). In some cases they were perhaps merely collected by man, but probably in many cases partially, or wholly, artificially shaped. They would, of course, make very excellent sling or "bolas" stones. Here, too, the discovery near Heilbron in the Transvaal of a number of stone balls showing vertical grooves might be mentioned (8). They are, however, unassociated with any industry and the age of the culture to which these extraordinary objects should be assigned cannot therefore be determined with any certainty. Occasionally, too, pointed tools resembling *coups de poing* but made on flakes, the under surfaces being the flake surfaces, appear (Fig. VIII, 1). In North Africa too they have been found fairly frequently and it may be that they are due to the influence of a later (Middle Palaeolithic) culture.

Another distinctive type of tool common in Stellenbosch

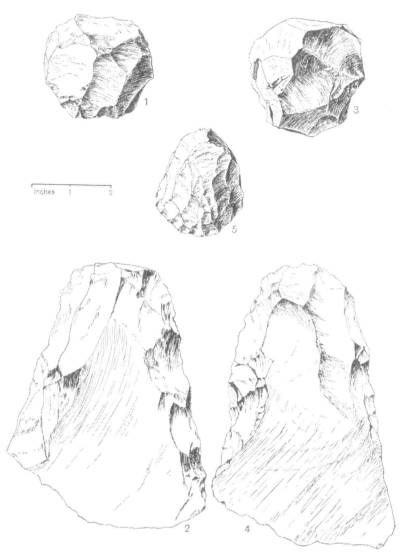

Fig. VII. 1. Roughly trimmed stone ball from Middledrift, C.P. 2. Stellenbosch cleaver from Villiersdorp, C.P. 3, 4. Similar tools for comparison from Tabelbala, Southern Algeria. 5. Chipped cone-shaped core from Middledrift, C.P.

industries is the cleaver (Fig. VII, 2 and Fig. IX, 1). In shape it reminds one of a large Campigny axe[1], for the working edge is straight or only slightly curved and is more or less at right angles to the length of the tool, being formed by the intersection of two large flake-scars slightly inclined to each other. This edge is at what in a normal *coup de poing* would be the butt end of the tool; the more pointed end is left blunt and sometimes some of the crust of the original pebble from which the tool was made remains. The whole gives one the impression that the tool was made by a similar technique as the *coup de poing* of which it is undoubtedly a near relative. The straight working edge often measures more than half as much as the complete length of the implement. It is quite clear that these cleavers, which were possibly hafted, were used as heavy chopping tools, and they must have been really very effective for this purpose. It is equally obvious that their absence from the Lower Palaeolithic industries of Europe is at once explained by the difference of the material used for making tools in the two continents. With any substance of a flinty nature an edge produced by the intersection of two large flake surfaces slightly inclined to one another would be far too brittle for use, except in the case of very small tools or for comparatively delicate work. Also it would not be at all easy to produce such a long more or less straight edge. Made from quartzite, however, which is essentially a tough material, they form effective implements and were easily made. They are of common occurrence in North Africa, however, and I myself possess in my collection many specimens (Fig. VII, 4) from the oasis of Tabelbala in Southern Algeria. Both in North and South Africa their association with ordinary pear-shaped and oval *coups de poing* fixes the industries and culture to which they belong.

Implements showing a new and interesting technique have been observed among the Pniel and Vaal river industries(21) and elsewhere (Figs. VIII, 2 and IX, 2). Some authors claim that these variants, as we may call them, are so distinctive as to warrant

[1] No connection between the tools, still less between their parent cultures, is in any way implied.

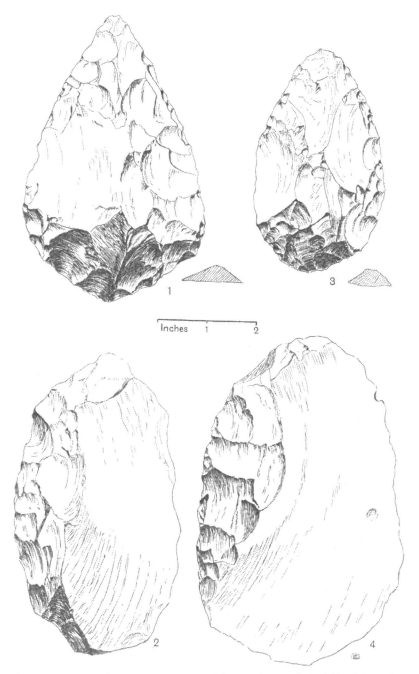

Fig. VIII. 1, 3. Pointed tools made on flakes, 1 from Middledrift, C.P., 3 from Tachenshit, Southern Algeria. 2, 4. Good examples of the special Pniel or Vaal river technique, 2 from Inyati river, S. Rhodesia, 4 from Tabelbala, S. Algeria.

their being raised to the dignity of distinct industries though still belonging to the Lower Palaeolithic culture. Though as just mentioned implements made with this special technique are of common occurrence in the gravels of the Vaal river, particularly near the old German mission station at Pniel a dozen miles or so from Kimberley, they are also frequently seen in the Stellenbosch industry at Mossel Bay on the one hand, and are found with *coups de poing* in river gravels in Southern Rhodesia on the other. It would therefore seem that this technique was found useful in the making of *coups de poing* from quartzites and other special materials, and that it is not a question of a really distinct industry which should be classed by itself. When an industry is recognised as distinct either a difference in age between it and other industries belonging to the same culture is implied, or else a definite geographical distribution proper to itself alone. It is, for example, for the latter reason that the Victoria West industry has been described separately; it has a special and limited geographical distribution. But the Pniel or Vaal river variants are found in many widely separated localities in the Union of South Africa as well as in Southern Rhodesia associated with regular Stellenbosch industries, and it is therefore impossible to separate them from these industries. At Pniel itself they are found among quite normal *coups de poing* made from the same material.

The mode of procedure when making a tool of the Pniel or Vaal river variant type seems to have been as follows. A large lump of quartzite was chosen, on the upper side of which a more or less flat surface was produced by a normal flaking process. From the under side a large flake inclined at a slight angle to the upper surface was then knocked off in such a way that the newly-formed flake surface intersected the flat trimmed surface producing one of the sharp edges of the tool. A certain amount of trimming, either to a pear-shaped or an oval form, then followed, and finally the portion between the bulb of percussion of the flake and other edge of the upper trimmed surface was boldly flaked, producing a narrow trimmed surface oblique to both the first two surfaces. The cross-section of such a tool is a narrow scalene triangle. Fig. VIII, 2 is a drawing of such a tool, showing the narrow, trimmed surface and the flake surface. The under surface, which is not shown, is more or less flat and flaked all over in the ordinary way. A further modification of this technique is found where both the lower and the upper surfaces are flake surfaces, showing bulbs of percussion and intersecting to form a sharp edge. Opposite to this edge there is a boldly trimmed surface as before, and the cross-section is again triangular, this trimming forming the third, steep and shortest side of the figure. This method is particularly ingenious as much labour is saved and a very efficient tool results. Sometimes the two flake surfaces do not intersect but are parallel, in which case both edges are trimmed back and the cross-section is a parallelogram. This method of trimming the edges is known in South Africa as reversed flaking and is sometimes used in the manufacture of the cleaver (Fig. IX, 2) which also occurs among the Vaal river variants. Whereas its more typically Stellenbosch relative described above has more or less sharp sides like an ordinary *coup de poing*, here the trimming definitely squares off the edges giving the tool a central cross-section which is a rectangle or more often a parallelogram and reminding one vaguely of a Danish axe.

The Pniel or Vaal river variant is by no means confined to South Africa. A great many examples of it have been collected from North Africa (Fig. VIII, 4), especially in the Tabelbala (49) district of South Algeria, and they are found just in an area where a similar kind of quartzite material had been utilised by prehistoric man for his tools. The technique of the Vaal river variant, however, would not be suitable for work in flint, as the edges so produced would not be very serviceable in the more brittle material. Hence, perhaps, its absence in European industries.

In the gravels of the Vaal river, associated with these peculiar tools, are also a number of long flakes without secondary working; these occasionally show a prepared striking platform. They may indicate the presence of a Middle Palaeolithic influence; we know from Professor Seligman's work (43)

that the Mousterians penetrated into North Africa and probably
survived there for a very long time; they also certainly reached
Uganda (51).

In the figures which illustrate the various Stellenbosch tool
types I have sometimes added for purposes of comparison
drawings of the same types from North Africa. The similarity
is astounding.

THE FAURESMITH INDUSTRIES (Fig. x)

The Fauresmith industries, as the name implies, are found
centred around the little town of Fauresmith in the Orange
Free State. Implements can be collected there both on the
surface of the ground and in the dry river bed as well as in
the gravels forming the river bank. Another good site, not far
from Fauresmith itself, is on the left of the road to Koffiefontein,
just before the homestead of the farm called Brakfontein is
reached. There a donga seems to have cut through an ancient
dune, and many beautiful Fauresmith tools can be found. Close
by, too, some rather soft marls, probably of no great antiquity,
have been laid down, and from a depth of 2 feet in this deposit
Fauresmith implements have been collected.

The essential feature of the industries is the number of finely
made *coups de poing*, usually smaller in size than those found in
the Stellenbosch industries. They are frequently made from
indurated shale; a very fine workmanship is possible and the
resulting tools rival anything found in Acheulean or early
Mousterian industries in Europe. One implement from Brakfon-
tein, for instance, is about 5 inches long by $2\frac{1}{2}$ inches wide (maximum dimensions). It is boldly flaked all over, the butt end being
sharp and the general shape is that of an isosceles triangle with
a rounded base. The edges show considerable secondary working,
one being sharper than the other. A certain amount of the
S-twist is present. The whole forms a really lovely object (Fig.
x, 2). A very similar example was collected by us from the
gravels at the town-spruit of Fauresmith itself, and still another
found near Bloemfontein, is rather squatter and flatter for its
size, but equally beautiful in workmanship (Fig x, 3). Some of

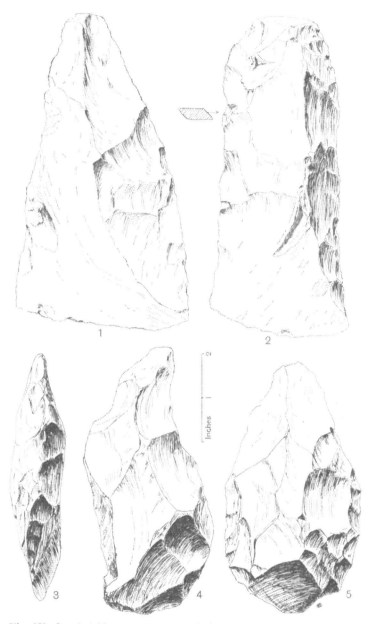

Fig. IX. South African Lower Palaeolithic tools. 1. Excellent example of a Stellenbosch cleaver from Middledrift. 2. Cleaver with parallelogram section showing the Pniel or Vaal river technique, from Pniel. 3. Twisted ovate from Pniel. 4. Variety of *coup de poing* from Middledrift. 5. Typical Stellenbosch *coup de poing* from Mossel Bay.

the smaller triangular *coups de poing* remind one of the Combe Capelle type in Europe, a comparison made all the more interesting by the fact that a number of triangular flakes (Fig. X, 1), also made from indurated shale, heavily patinated and showing a prepared or faceted striking platform, although often without secondary working up the edges, have been found in the Fauresmith industry. These triangular flakes with their sharp tips very closely resemble European Mousterian points. The absence of trimming up the sides so frequently observed may merely be due to the nature of the material; the toughening process resulting from fine resolved trimming is unnecessary in the case of the already fairly tough indurated shale to the same extent as in that of flint or flinty materials.

Some small side-scrapers showing resolved flaking as well as some disc-like tools, have been collected from Brakfontein and elsewhere. If found in Europe the whole industry would be classed as either belonging to the end of the Acheulean or to the beginning of the Mousterian culture. Unfortunately there is as yet no instance in South Africa of a stratigraphical sequence between typical Stellenbosch and Fauresmith industries, and we cannot therefore state definitely that the Fauresmith is later in time than the Stellenbosch, although every indication points to this being the case. Indeed it seems more than probable that a strong Middle Palaeolithic influence can be traced in the exceedingly beautiful and interesting Fauresmith industry. Therefore while at present classing it, as has heretofore been done, in the Lower Palaeolithic culture, I feel, in view of what will be said shortly about the Middle Palaeolithic influence in South Africa, that it is by no means certain that it should not rather be classed as Middle Palaeolithic in culture.

The reader may be inclined to enquire why it has not been found possible in South Africa to distinguish in the Lower Palaeolithic culture industries comparable to the Chellean and Acheulean of Europe. It has been pointed out that both roughly made *coups de poing* as well as finer examples showing the S-shaped twist occur, and also the oval variety so characteristic of Acheulean industries in the north. No doubt some

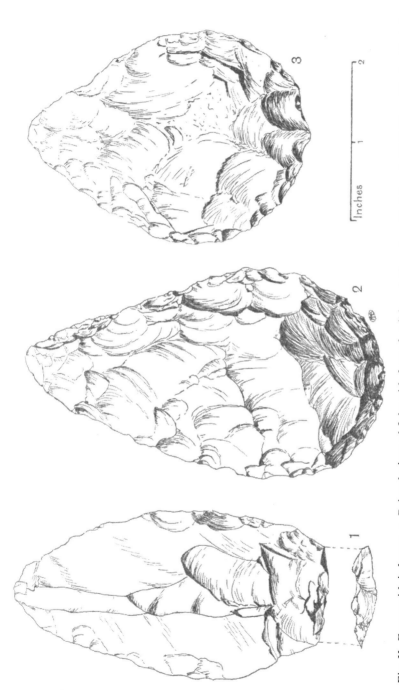

Fig. X. Fauresmith industry. 1. Pointed trimmed flake with faceted striking platform from Brakfontein (O.F.S.). 2. Finely chipped *coup de poing* from Brakfontein (O.F.S.). 3. Small *coup de poing* from Bloemfontein.

such subdivision will be possible eventually, but at present both rough and fine varieties are found together on surface sites and in the two lower gravel terraces of some of the rivers. As a result it is not possible to distinguish separate industries with any certainty. Again, with such refractory material as quartzite, the personal skill of the implement-maker must have played a much more important part in determining the shape of the tool than is the case with flint, which so readily lends itself to tool-making purposes. What we should like to find are a number of localities where these implements occur in stratigraphical relationship with one another, as happens in Europe in the gravels of the Somme Valley, etc. At Stellenbosch itself we did find *coups de poing in situ* as described above. But there was no time or means to undertake extensive exploration or to determine whether or not any sequence of types could be observed.

At Montagu Cave (19), near Ashton (C.P.), however, below a Wilton industry, Mr Goodwin has found several Stellenbosch industries separated by sterile layers. It has been definitely proved at this site that the pear-shaped *coups de poing* (including some immense examples discovered there) are older than the flatter and more oval forms, which never appear in the lower layers. This, of course, is in exact accord with the European sequence; but, before any definite statement can be made, further localities where a stratigraphy of Lower Palaeolithic industries exists must be explored. My own belief is that the situation is really analogous to that in Europe, namely that there existed an earlier Lower Palaeolithic, i.e. Chellean stock, the pre-Chellean stage being perhaps absent, and that later, Acheulean developments were introduced or developed *in situ* on parallel lines, with the really astounding result that exactly similar industries occur in both regions. As a matter of fact, most of the Lower Palaeolithic implements found in South Africa would, in Europe, be classed as Acheulean. The names Chellean and Acheulean are not particularly happy, more especially in view of the fact that the one thing almost absent from the gravels at Chelles-sur-Marne is the Chellean *coup de poing*, practically all the tools found there belonging to the Acheulean culture!

However, they are names sanctioned by long usage and they are of world-wide acceptance. It would be difficult to replace them and such an attempt would be likely to lead to confusion without any benefit accruing. For the present, therefore, it is probably wiser in South Africa to stick to the larger term Lower Palaeolithic culture, using the local names for subdivisions.

CHAPTER V

MIDDLE PALAEOLITHIC INFLUENCES
AND THE FIRST APPEARANCE
OF NEOANTHROPIC MAN

I N the last chapter we gave a description of the Fauresmith industries and stated that a number of pointed flakes showing faceted striking platforms were associated with finely made, sometimes triangular, *coups de poing*. It was suggested that a Middle Palaeolithic influence must have come into contact with the older Lower Palaeolithic culture. I believe this to have been the case, though nowhere, as far as has been yet discovered, can a purely Middle Palaeolithic industry be seen, although, typologically speaking, Middle Palaeolithic tools can often be noted. The most nearly pure Middle Palaeolithic industries that we came across were found at the small site below the Glengrey Falls, not very far from Queenstown (Plate III). The spot is rich in prehistoric tools (Fig. XI). Among the implements found were a number of pointed flakes with faceted striking platforms, but with the sides mostly left untrimmed (Fig. XI, 2). These correspond exactly to those found in the Fauresmith industries. But there was also one example, long and slender, showing beautiful resolved flaking down each side, as well as a faceted striking platform. The specimen is fairly heavily patinated (Fig. XI, 1). If this tool had been found in the Upper Mousterian levels at La Quina, France, it would have been passed without remark, excepting that the material (indurated shale) would have made it conspicuous. At the Glengrey site a number of discs (Fig. XI, 5 and 6) were also found, as well as tools which might be described as roughly-made Levallois flakes. No side-scrapers, however, were collected. On the other hand, several core-scrapers (Fig. XI, 3), rarely found in Europe before Upper Palaeolithic times, were noticed. It was interesting, too, to find here a small pebble, sharpened along one edge, and clearly intended to form a miniature chopping tool (Fig. XI, 4).

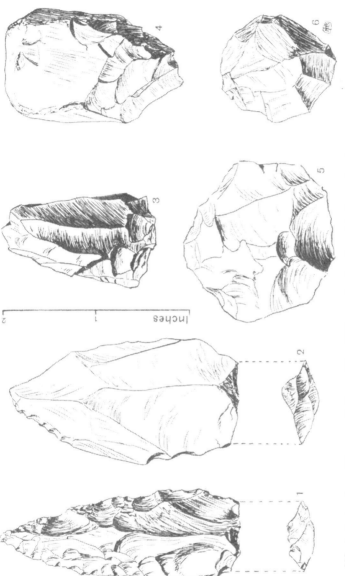

Fig. XI. Industry from Glengrey Falls. 1. Fine "Mousterian" point with faceted striking platform. 2. Ditto, less well worked. 3. Rough core-scraper. 4. Small chopping tool. 5. Disc. 6. Small round scraping tool made on a flake

The tools illustrated in Fig. XII were collected from Yardley, near Sterkstroom. The first is a typical side-scraper made on a flake, the bulb being at one end without any prepared striking platform. The working edge is slightly convex and is trimmed by resolved flaking. The tool is rather more weather-worn than the magnificent point already described from the Glengrey Falls site. The other two specimens are also what in Europe would be called Mousterian points. The longer example is made from a flake struck off from a carefully prepared striking platform. Both sides have been trimmed, the edges intersecting at the tip. The third specimen is considerably thicker, there is a bulb with no prepared striking platform and the edges are trimmed with fine resolved flaking, producing a sharp-pointed tool.

In the pan at Alexandersfontein near Kimberley (p. 33) heavily patinated discs and tools, recalling in shape Middle Palaeolithic types, occur. One of these latter is 4 inches long by 2 inches across (maximum dimensions) and shows a good bulb with *éraillure* and well-prepared striking platform. A certain amount of resolved trimming is seen on both sides, especially towards the tip which unfortunately is broken off.

Dr Van Hoepen has collected from Thaba N'chu, on the line from Bloemfontein to Bethlehem, an implement which in Europe would be accepted unhesitatingly as a typical Levallois flake. It is made from indurated shale and is more or less un-patinated, although found on the surface. The find was isolated and cannot therefore with certainty be assigned to any culture, but, from a typological point of view, it was made either by Middle Palaeolithic man himself[1], or by folk who at some period or other had been influenced by him. Further north, in Southern Rhodesia, the same state of affairs exists, and both at Saw-mills (33) and near the Victoria Falls implements of a Middle Palaeolithic type in appearance and technique have been

---

[1] As has already been pointed out, cultures in South Africa may be more recent in time than the corresponding cultures in Europe. It is quite possible that the Middle Palaeolithic culture survived long in North Africa and only penetrated into South Africa at a comparatively late date.

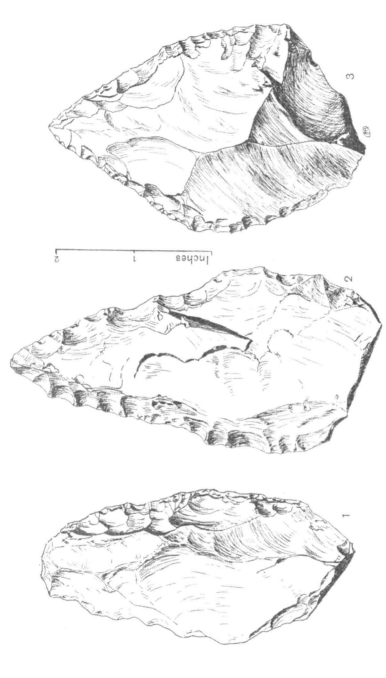

Inches

Fig. XII. Industry from Yardley, near Sterkstroom, C.P. 1. Side scraper. 2, 3. Large "Mousterian" points.

collected. At the Victoria Falls sites we tried to determine whether a sorting and grouping purely on grounds of patina and preservation would be found to separate the Middle Palaeolithic from the Lower Palaeolithic types of tools. The result, although not conclusive, tended to show that the typical Lower Palaeolithic tools were the more heavily patinated and therefore the older. But the state of preservation to-day is necessarily a capricious factor in determining age, as has already been stated earlier in this volume. It is of little use, except locally, and when the industries in question have been long studied and the conditions of the site are well known.

An interesting implement which has been discovered in the Lichtenberg alluvial diamond workings is now preserved in the Pretoria Museum[1]. It consists of an oval flake some 5 inches long by $3\frac{1}{2}$ inches wide and 1 inch thick at its maximum. There is a conspicuous bulb, but no striking platform. Both sides have been carefully trimmed, resolved flaking being employed. The result is a sort of double side-scraper of a distinctly Mousterian appearance.

At a number of other sites mixed industries occur, as for example at Rockwood Farm near Queenstown; at Middledrift (C.P.); at Cofimvaba (Transkei); and at the site close to the Process bridge, O.F.S. (p. 39). *Coups de poing*, or what appear at first sight to be *coups de poing*, are found, but a closer examination shows that their under sides are flake surfaces (Fig. VIII, 1). This again demonstrates that a Middle Palaeolithic influence must have been acting on a Lower Palaeolithic culture. As regards the relative age of these apparently Middle Palaeolithic types of tools, an interesting site has been found by Mr Neville Jones in the spruit at Taungs (33), where such tools were found in a thin deposit, but a few inches thick, resting upon a thick deposit containing Lower Palaeolithic implements. On the surface of the ground outside the spruit Smithfield tools occurred and we thus obtain a sequence: Lower Palaeolithic, Middle Palaeolithic, Smithfield.

[1] The Curator very kindly permitted me to make a cast of it, which is now in the Museum of Archaeology and Ethnology at Cambridge.

Middle Palaeolithic industries have been found at many sites in North Africa. Some very beautiful Mousterian points come from Somaliland; they show a deep white patina similar to that seen on Lower Palaeolithic tools from the same district.

We now turn our attention to Neoanthropic man in South Africa. That he existed there is undoubted, and the similarity of some industries to those discovered by Mr Leakey at Elementeita in Kenya is complete. In this connection the most important site yet discovered is near Grahamstown at Howieson's Poort, where the excavations are due to the energy of Mr Hewitt and Father Stapleton (46).

The industry (Fig. XIII) at this site includes a very large number of flakes which by no means resemble those found at the more modern Wilton sites in the neighbourhood, being far more archaic in appearance. Besides these some discs occur and also some large crescents, the blunting on the back of which is confined to a short extent at each extremity and does not occur along the back of the tool opposite the working edge (Fig. XIII, 2). There was also found a leaf-shaped flake finely trimmed all over the upper surface and recalling somewhat tools found in the Still Bay industries. But besides these tools, eight perfect burins have been unearthed (Fig. XIII, 5–9). In Europe burins first appear in Upper Palaeolithic or rather in Aurignacian times. They form a group of very distinctive tools. The characteristic feature of a burin is that it has a facet left when a flake is removed by a vertical blow delivered down the side of the implement while the implement itself is held vertical. Generally this facet cuts off part of one edge of the implement, converting the tip, which may perhaps have been the flat point of a flake, into a square edge like a screwdriver instead of a penknife. There are many ways of preparing the other side of the implement which intersects the burin facet, but the essential thing is this peculiar facet itself which runs always more or less down the length of the implement and more or less truncates the edge of the original flake. The burins at Howieson's Poort are typically Upper Palaeolithic in appearance and belong to various types; the "ordinary" burin occurs where the burin facet is backed against another burin facet; also the "angle" burin where the burin facet is backed against a trimmed edge; also a "single-blow" burin where the burin facet is backed against the broken end of a blade. The finds are unlike anything so far discovered in South Africa, with the exception of one burin unearthed by Mr Neville Jones at Sawmills[1], but they can be matched tool by tool from the industries at Elementeita in Kenya[2]. Similar burins, too, are of common occurrence in the Capsian industries of North Africa. I am strongly of the opinion that other similar discoveries will soon be made in South Africa, and that these tools were due to an early migration thither of Neoanthropic man. By what route the migration took place is completely unknown; perhaps the province of Natal, ground as yet little touched by the archaeologist, will some day have a tale to tell.

It is quite possible that in Southern Rhodesia a rather indeterminate industry found in the lower levels at the Cave of Bambata (Matopo Hills) (1) is also to be connected with this culture. It is possible, too, that it was these folk who introduced the practice of art and that the earlier series of paintings in Southern Rhodesia were their handiwork, at some period before they penetrated further into what is now the Union. If this be the case it would seem that they sojourned in the north for a considerable time before they migrated further southwards in large numbers. Possibly the occupation of the land by the folk belonging to previous migrations prevented them from continuing their southward trek until further pressure from the north made some movement imperative. Should this be so, a very close link has been forged between the studies of the industries and art of these people in South Africa, and similar studies of Upper Palaeolithic cultures in North Africa and

---

[1] Among the immense number of Smithfield implements so far collected two burin-like tools alone have been detected. The resemblance is, however, only fortuitous ; such pseudo-burins have occasionally been found in industries of every culture and at all times.

[2] The tools illustrated on Fig. xx, 2 should be mentioned in this connection. They come from Kenya, not far from Lake Naivasha.

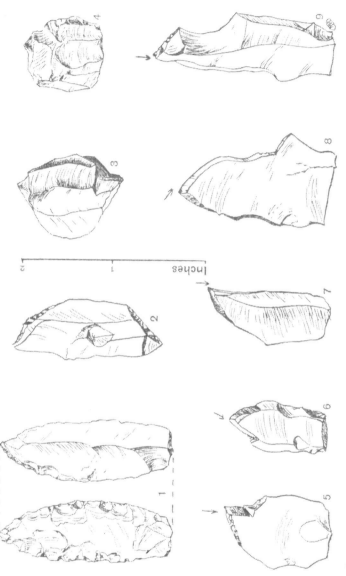

Fig. XIII. Industry from Howieson's Poort. 1. Back and front of a flake trimmed all over one surface. 2. Large crescent, the chipping not continuing all round the back. 3, 4. Small core-scrapers. 5, 6, 7, 8, 9. Varieties of burins.

Europe[1]. Mr Leakey's researches in Kenya are definitely proving the thesis which had long been held by many, viz. that the areas of North Africa now desert, but formerly at the end of Quaternary times fertile lands, were the cradle of the Neoanthropic race. There is little doubt that from this cradle various modifications of the original stock, whatever it was, migrated in all directions, especially on the commencement of the drying-up process of the land, which has, with several fluctuations, finally led to the desert conditions prevailing to-day.

We must now glance at the Still Bay industries, which seem to me to be due to the contact of Neoanthropic man with the people among whom he found himself in South Africa.

THE STILL BAY CULTURE (Fig. xiv)

Tools belonging to the Still Bay culture were early recognised as artefacts in South Africa. In fact they were included among some of the earliest tools sent to London towards the middle of last century. It is only lately, however, that the culture itself has been clearly distinguished and that a number of industries belonging to it have been investigated. The type station is at the mouth of the Kafferkuils river, some twenty-three miles south of Riversdale in the Cape Province. Unfortunately there is no stratigraphy to be studied; all the sites are on the surface and not only do we find there a Still Bay industry, but Lower Palaeolithic, Wilton, and Kitchen Midden industries as well. To a certain extent, however, the distribution of the various industries is restricted and those belonging to the Still Bay culture are more or less confined to the seaward slope of a limy ridge which cuts across the country from the Indian Ocean at one end to a mile or two up the right bank of the river-estuary on the other (p. 50).

Besides a number of flakes and discs a typical tool occurs in the Still Bay industries. It is a sort of laurel leaf, and consists of a blade pointed at one or both ends, flat compared with its length, and trimmed over both surfaces, pressure-flaking

[1] See bibliography (20); I personally do not consider that the Smithfield culture is to be classed as Upper Palaeolithic.

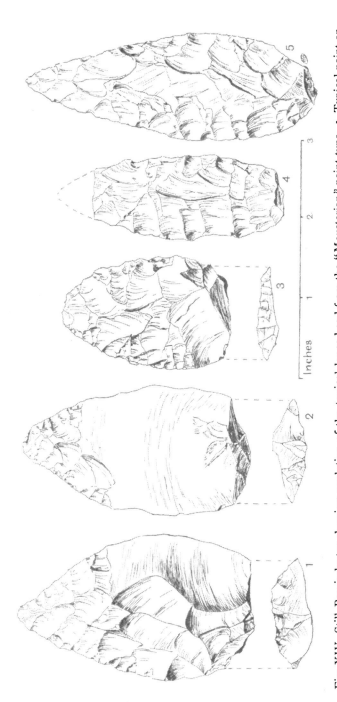

Fig. XIV. Still Bay industry showing evolution of the typical lance head from the "Mousterian" point type. 1. Typical point on flake with faceted striking platform from Fish Hoek, C.P. 2. Ditto, with thinning flaking on under surface at tip from Fish Hoek. 3. Ditto, trimmed all over both surfaces from Noord Hoek, C.P. 4. Typical Still Bay lance head from Still Bay. 5. Ditto, locality uncertain. Bulbs of percussion and the striking platform of 4 and 5 have been practically all chipped away.

being often employed. The flake scars are often narrow with parallel sides, and the flaking is of the nature of fluting. Occasionally only one side has been so flaked, the under surface being the primary flake surface. Such tools must have formed very effective lance points, quite strong if the blow given were direct, although liable to be smashed owing to their thinness if the blow struck were oblique. They could penetrate between the shoulder-blades of an ox, in the same way as in the bull-ring to-day the matador's sword pierces its victim. The folk so armed would have a more serviceable weapon than those having only such a weapon as, for example, the Mousterian point.

The evolution, in South Africa, of this laurel-leaf type of javelin head from the "Mousterian" point has been clearly demonstrated by Col. Hardy[1], who has collected a number of tools showing such a development. This can readily be seen by reference to Fig. XIV. In the first instance we have a typical point, the lower surface being a flake with good bulb of percussion and *éraillure*; there is also a well-prepared striking platform. The upper surface is trimmed and the edges, trimmed by resolved flaking, intersect in a sharp tip. The second specimen is in every sense a duplicate of the first, except that near the tip the under flake surface has been further thinned by the removal of scales of material by pressure flaking. In the third instance almost the whole of both the upper and lower surfaces are thus treated by pressure flaking, and there results a tool which is very thin relative to its size. The bulb and prepared striking platform, however, still remain. Finally we have the finished product, the true Still Bay lance head, in which the bulb and striking platform have disappeared in the process of completely pressure flaking the tool all over (Fig. XIV, 4 and 5). It is interesting to note that a very similar evolution from the "Mousterian" point has been detected by Mr Leakey in Kenya and can also be seen in North Africa in an area where, in all probability, Mousterian man was in contact with Capsian man (i.e. Aurignacian man in North Africa). It is quite possible

[1] A partial account of Col. Hardy's most interesting collections from near Cape Town has been published by Mr Goodwin, bibliography (18).

that the true Solutrean culture itself developed in Hungary as the result of a similar contact between Neoanthropic and Mousterian peoples on the edge of the Neoanthropic world. Should this be so we shall have to admit that these pressure-flaked lance heads, which have such a wide distribution, are not "type fossils" of the Solutrean culture, which itself is confined solely to an area north of the Alps and Pyrenees, but are an indication of contact between Middle Palaeolithic and Upper Palaeolithic cultures. Why such contact should produce these lance heads, it is perhaps not easy to say, but the fact that both in South Africa and in North Africa series can be collected showing such an evolution is very significant.

An important site is a cave between Fish Hoek and Noord Hoek (Plate III), at present being excavated by Mr Peers and his son. Rich Still Bay finds occur under six feet of Kitchen Midden material and there is therefore a stratigraphical sequence, which shows the Still Bay to be the earlier of the two industries. The site is especially interesting, as the Still Bay tools are not sand polished, as is always the case when they are found in open sand-dune country. It is further significant that in these Still Bay industries there has been found a skull which is very different in type from the usual Bushman remains, such as are found with Wilton and Kitchen Midden industries. That the Still Bay industries are older than those belonging to the Wilton culture can be often demonstrated by the fact that, where the two industries occur together on the same settlement site, the weathering of the Still Bay tools is always the deeper, and also because in several instances Wilton tools have been discovered made from older Still Bay flakes. That is to say, the Wilton folk discovered the Still Bay tools and flakes lying about and utilised them for the purpose of making their own implements.

In distribution the true Still Bay culture is restricted, practically speaking, to the south coasts of the continent. Occasional isolated finds of the lance head type are not necessarily indicative of the presence of the true Still Bay culture, as has been already explained above. I am inclined to think that the

Neoanthropic culture, which gave rise to the Howieson's Poort industry, played a not inconsiderable part in the evolution of the Still Bay culture and that therefore we are justified in comparing to a certain extent the industry at Howieson's Poort with Still Bay industries. It is more than probable that in the extreme south of the continent, where further migration southward by the folk of earlier cultures was stopped by the ocean, hybridisation with the Neoanthropic people took place and that the Still Bay culture was a derivative of such a hybridisation of Neoanthropic and Lower Palaeolithic elements which had already been subjected to Middle Palaeolithic influences as already suggested at the beginning of this chapter.

CHAPTER VI

THE LATER CULTURES

THREE more cultures and their industries remain to be considered. They were listed in Chapter I and are called respectively the Wilton, Smithfield and Kitchen Midden cultures.

THE WILTON CULTURE (Fig. xv)

The Wilton culture, so named after the type station 35 miles from Grahamstown, excavated by Mr Hewitt and Father Stapleton (26) (28), was undoubtedly brought into South Africa by a new people coming from the north. Similar industries are known in Uganda (as the Magozi culture) and in Kenya. In Southern Rhodesia it is found in a very pure state, associated with the later series of rock-shelter paintings developed there. The industries consist almost entirely of pigmy tools. These include small lunates or crescents, pointed needle-like tools whose sides are trimmed with minute flaking, blunted-backs, small thumbnail-scrapers, and core-scrapers, etc. The tool-making skill of the Wilton people was very considerable. At Gokomere (Fort Victoria, Southern Rhodesia) the industries are made almost entirely from clear quartz, and as one studies the hundreds of delicate little lunates manufactured from this most intractable material, one is at a loss to imagine how they could have been made. Mr Leakey suggests that the ordinary lunate was fashioned by taking a chip, holding it against the end of one's thumb, and then rounding and blunting the back by the removal of a number of small flakes by a chipping process; certainly the curve of the blunted back of the lunate is in many cases not dissimilar to that of the end of one's thumb or finger. It is necessary to postulate that some such easy method must have been employed in order to account for the thousands of such tools found.

Quite clearly none of these tiny pigmies could have been used by themselves as implements, so the Wilton folk must have already learnt the advantages of using a composite tool—that is to say, a tool the working edge of which is made from one or more suitably chipped stones which are hafted on to some softer or lighter material, such as wood or bone[1]. Only certain shapes of pigmies would be suitable or useful for thus forming a working edge. These can be seen on reference to Fig. XV, where suggested methods of hafting a number of lunates to form quite an effective knife blade and barbed arrow head (Fig. XV, 45 and 46) are also shown. It is possible, too, that a number of the finer and more needle-like points which occur in Wilton industries, besides being used as awls for the manufacture of ostrich egg-shell beads, etc., may have been hafted together through a thin flat piece of wood or other substance, in such a way that the points just projected through the mount. The resulting tool would be very useful in the softening and working up of skins preparatory to making clothes, etc.

Ostrich egg-shell beads are frequently found. The earlier examples seem to have been made by chipping fragments of ostrich egg shell to a more or less suitable size (Fig. XV, 37 and 38), piercing them and then smoothing and making them circular by snipping off fragments all round. In later times, as a final process, the roughly made beads seem to have been strung tightly together and rubbed down in a grooved stone, of which examples are frequently found both in Wilton and Smithfield industries, until perfect little flat ring beads resulted. In Wilton industries beads made from other materials than ostrich egg shell have also been found, and in one instance it is claimed that a bead of Roman date was found together with industries

---

[1] Father Gardner, of the Mission Station of Gokomere, suggests that they were used as arrow-barbs (Fig. XV, 45).

Fig. XV. Wilton pigmy industry. 1–3. Small core-scrapers. 4–10. Crescents. 11–13. Thumbnail-scrapers. 14–19. Double crescents. 20–23. Small scrapers. 24, 25 and 27–29. Blunted backs. 26 and 40. Awls. 30–34. Crescents. 35, 36. Tattooing points(?). 37–39. Ostrich egg-shell beads. 41–44. Fragments of pottery and a scraper. 45, 46. Suggested methods of hafting crescents. 1–29. From Cape Flats except 11, 22 and 29 from Wilton and 10 from Riversdale; 30–35 from Gokomere, Fort Victoria, S. Rhodesia; 36 from Sawmills, S. Rhodesia; 37–39 from Wilton; 40 from Riverton; 41–44 from Middledrift.

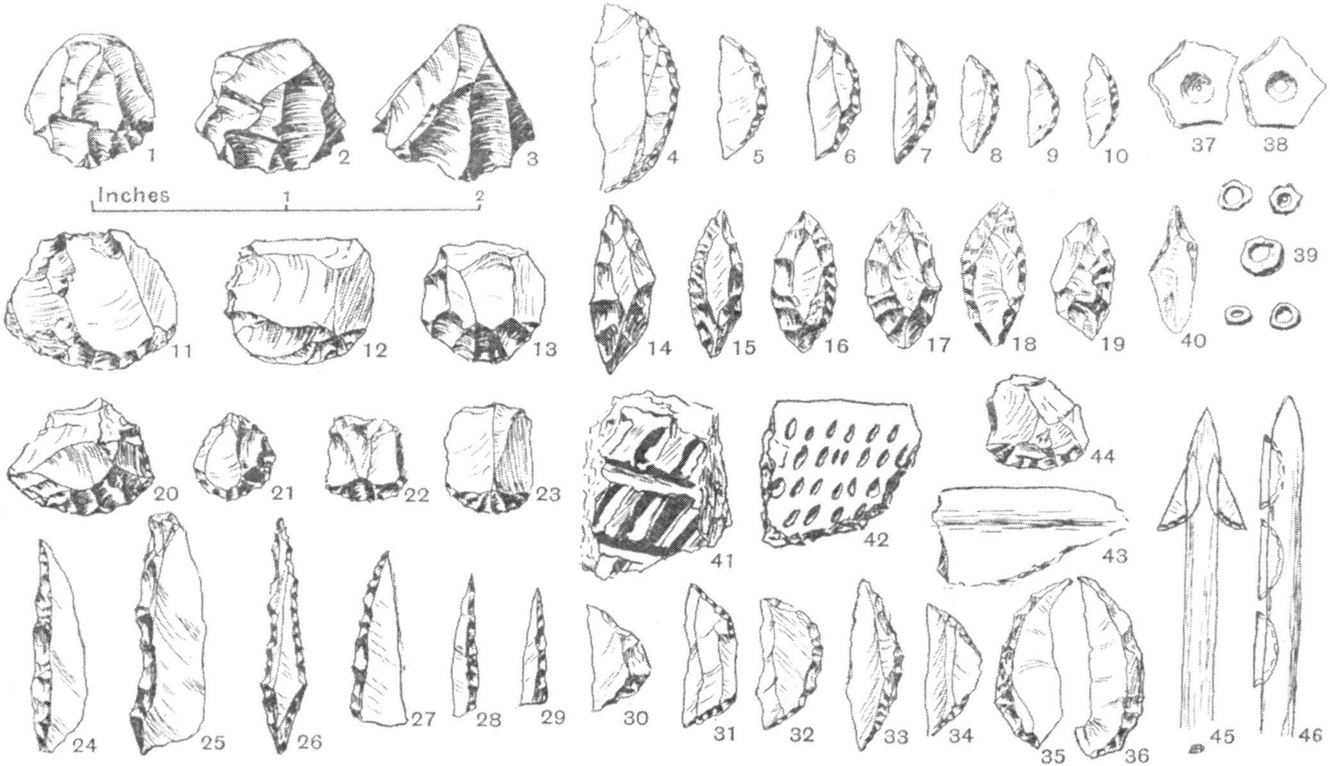

Fig. XV.

belonging to a Wilton culture. It is quite possible that this was so, and it would seem probable that the Wilton culture endured for a very long period in time and perhaps may embrace more than one migration from the north. The Wilton folk also knew how to make rough pottery, and bone tools, chiefly awls, are known; the material is usually still fairly fresh, that is to say the organic matter has not all been leached out and the bone fossilised. A few peculiar slate objects, recalling, though on a smaller scale, pre-dynastic Egyptian palettes, must be noted. Occasionally their edges are denticulated. These palettes so far have only been found in the Grahamstown district (28). There is at least one example of a chisel-like tool the working edge of which is made by a polishing technique[1]. It is now in the Albany Museum at Grahamstown.

Bored stones (Fig. XVIII) of varying size are also known, some being very large and heavy. These are stone balls pierced through the middle by a hole which is usually more or less splayed at both ends[2]. Such bored stones are still in use among the surviving remnant of the Bushmen who use them to weight their digging sticks. The latter consist of a stout stick passed through one of the bored stones which is held in place by a wedge below. The whole makes quite an effective crowbar-like implement.

Wilton industries are found in Southern Rhodesia and thence sporadically as far south as Kimberley. They seem to be absent throughout most of the Orange Free State[3], where their place is apparently taken by the Smithfield industries, with which, in all probability, they were contemporary. They are found, however, south and east of the mountains, being common in the Grahamstown district and, of course, at the type site Wilton[4]. Along the south coast they are frequently found and

[1] See p. 102 and note in this connection.

[2] Various types of bored stones can be determined. They have been studied by Mr Van Riet Lowe and his results will be published shortly.

[3] However Major Collins long ago collected some small Wilton scrapers near Harrismith.

[4] A number of interesting implements, rather peculiar in type, have been found in the Eastern Province; it is not easy in all cases to assign them with confidence to definite cultures (27), (29).

occur in profusion in the Cape Peninsula, where, in their final evolution, an amazingly high standard of tool-making technique is attained.

Many sites have been investigated around Capetown; those near the Elsie river and at Noord Hoek are especially well known. We have already mentioned that Mr Peers and his son have been excavating an important rock-shelter near Fish Hoek; they have also investigated another not far off which has yielded a very nice Wilton industry.

At the Montagu cave (p. 74), Mr Goodwin has found Wilton tools in a layer resting on deposits containing *coups de poing* (19). This definitely dates the Wilton culture as being later than the Lower Palaeolithic industries, and the fact, as has been already mentioned, that Wilton man, living in districts where the Still Bay industries occurred, utilised the flakes left by his predecessors in the manufacture of his own small tools, demonstrates that it is also later than the Still Bay culture.

Wilton industries frequently occur in painted rock-shelters. The paintings are very different in style from the well-known examples which are associated with Smithfield industries. The problems of the paintings, however, will be discussed later on.

THE SMITHFIELD CULTURE (Figs. xvi, xvii and xviii)

The Smithfield culture is so called after the town of the same name in the Orange Free State where tools belonging to industries of this culture were collected long ago by Dr Kannemeyer. The name, however, is not particularly happy, as Smithfield itself seems to be nearer the edge than the centre of the area of distribution of the earlier industries of this culture.

Happily we know more about the Smithfield culture than any other, thanks largely to the tireless researches of Mr Van Riet Lowe, who has not only studied the industries in detail but has carefully mapped all the sites at present discovered in the Orange Free State.

The culture can be divided into two stages, an earlier and a later, known respectively as the Lower Smithfield and the Upper Smithfield. Mr Van Riet Lowe has lately come to the conclusion that the Smithfield industries found so often in rock-shelters with paintings can be distinguished, as a Smithfield C group, from the two above-mentioned divisions which he calls Smithfield A and B respectively. Personally I am not convinced that such a Smithfield C can be thus separated: I fancy the occurrence of thumbnail-scrapers, etc., in some of these industries merely indicates some contact with the Wilton culture. This view is substantiated if Mr Van Riet Lowe's excellent distribution map is studied, for sites where Smithfield C industries occur are on the eastern edge of the Smithfield world and are never very far from what probably was or had been Wilton country. The two-fold division has been found possible on typological grounds combined with evidence obtained from a study of the preservation of the tools occurring at the Smithfield site at De Kiel Oost, as already described in Chapter 1.

THE LOWER SMITHFIELD INDUSTRIES

The material used in Lower Smithfield industries is generally indurated shale. The implements include end-scrapers (generally known as "duck-bills"), circular scrapers, trimmed and used flakes, side-scrapers of a peculiar type, stone borers, trimmed points, trimming stones, etc. Duck-bill scrapers (Fig. XVI, 9) are of frequent occurrence, although not so numerous nor so neatly made as in Upper Smithfield industries. The sharp convex working edge at the end of the small blade is obtained by rough trimming and the sides of the tools are sometimes trimmed, sometimes left untrimmed. As a rule the curved working edge does not grade insensibly into the edges of the flake but two distinct shoulders are apparent. Apart from other considerations this fact distinguishes duck-bills from the vast majority of ordinary end-scrapers belonging to Upper Palaeolithic or Neolithic

Fig. XVI. Smithfield industries. 1. Grooved sandstone for shaping bone tools, etc. from De Kiel Oost (O.F.S.). 2. Concavo-convex scraper from Brakfontein (O.F.S.). 3, 4, 5, 6, 7. Small grinder, pierced stone, large chopper, scraper on flake, and awl, from De Kiel Oost (O.F.S.). 8. Pestle from near Molteno. 9. Scraper from Middledrift. 2 is typical of Lower Smithfield industries.

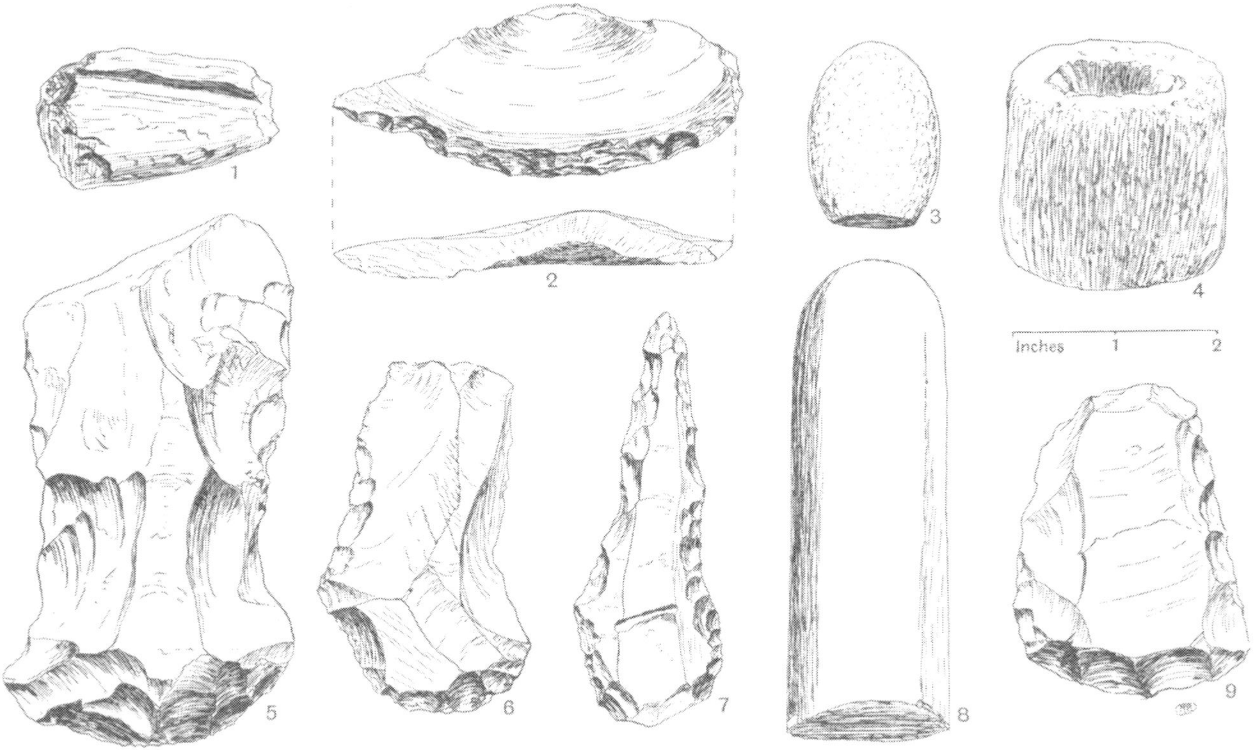

Fig. XVI.

cultures, where such shoulders are of rare occurrence. The circular scraper (Fig. XVII, 1 and 2) consists of a fair-sized circular or oval flake, trimmed most of the way round to form a sharp cutting edge, except where the bulb of percussion is. The side-scrapers of peculiar type (Fig. XVI, 2) are perhaps the most interesting and typical of the Lower Smithfield implements; they do not occur in Upper Smithfield industries. The type of tool consists of a flake showing a bulb of percussion in the middle of one side of the flake and not at one end as is usually the case. The upper side is formed by the striking off of another flake. The result is a flake with a positive bulb of percussion on the underside, and a flake surface showing a negative bulb of percussion on the upper side. The edge of the flake with the bulbs, therefore, is wavy, the upper surface being concave and the lower surface convex. The side opposite to the bulbs is neatly trimmed to a sharp, curved working edge. The name given to such an object is a concavo-convex side-scraper. The trimming for the most part shows resolved flaking and is almost Mousterian in appearance.

The borers vary considerably in size, some being of the nature of medium-sized awls, the pointed end being obtained by rough chipping all round (Fig. XVI, 7). Some large specimens occur, however, in appearance not so very unlike small Neolithic picks, such as are found in the Thames valley and elsewhere. In the case of one example, now in my possession, a sharp edge at the tip has been obtained by the removal of a flake with an almost burin-like technique. There is no reason, however, to consider this as anything but fortuitous. The trimmed points are of very great interest, recalling in general appearance Capsian points from North Africa. A blade is struck off showing the bulb of percussion and occasionally something of a faceted platform. One side is blunted for some distance from the tip towards the butt end, the other side remaining untrimmed and sharp to form the working edge or knife blade. These tools were presumably used in the same way as the Capsian, or Châtelperron points (Fig. II, 9) typical of Lower Aurignacian industries in France. Doubtless a finger was placed on the blunted portion in such a way that pressure could be applied to the sharp working edge opposite to it. A very nice example of this type of trimmed point was found by us on the commonage near Molteno, just above the railway station and between the railway and the native location. It is perfect in every way except that the extreme tip has been broken off (Fig. XVII, 23).

The trimming-stones (Fig. XVI, 5 and Fig. XVII, 3 and 4) vary in size and shape; a typical example is not unlike a large core-scraper. Mr Van Riet Lowe considers that they were used in the manufacture of duck-bills and other tools, in other words, that they are of the nature of hammer-stones. In such an area as South Africa, where ordinary rounded river pebbles are less in evidence than in Europe, hammer-stones would have to be made by flaking, and a sort of core-scraper with a flat flake surface below, from which rise a number of long flake scars, there being usually some undercutting, would be very suitable. But in this category, too, occur trimming-stones made from flat pieces of indurated shale, the ends of which have been trimmed. These, however, may also have been used as chopping tools. Sometimes the worked edge is convex, occasionally concave.

One or two instances are known of what can only be described as burins. None were found at De Kiel Oost[1], but at the Smithfield site near Victoria West we came across a very burin-like tool formed on the broken end of a tiny flake. In this instance the working edge seems to have been re-sharpened at a later date by the striking of another burin blow parallel to the first. The second facet, however, being shorter than its predecessor, a small portion of the former remains. However, when the enormous mass of Smithfield tools is considered, the occurrence of two or three burins becomes of little importance. Even in the Neolithic industries in Europe a few have been noted, and of course there is nothing to prevent a chance

[1] Mr Neville Jones had the good fortune at Alexandersfontein, near Kimberley, to find an excellent patinated example in indurated shale of an oblique, convex, angle burin. But there is no reason to date this find as Smithfield; the site has yielded industries of many ages and the tool is probably to be connected with the same culture as that of Howieson's Poort already described.

tool-maker belonging to any culture and of any age from employ-
ing the burin technique by accident. The important factor is not
that one or two burins occur, but that they are so extremely rare
compared with the quantity of material known, and this argues
strongly against Dr Van Hoepen's notion that the Smithfield
culture is to be correlated with the Upper Palaeolithic cultures
of Western Europe. Unfortunately it has not been possible to say
whether these one or two burin-like objects belong to Upper
or Lower Smithfield industries. It is equally difficult in the
case of a few engravings which have been found. These occur
either on a tool or on a chance piece of shale. An interesting
example showing a geometric pattern design was found by us
at De Kiel Oost (Fig. XVIII). In every case the engraving consists of a geometric pattern composed of meaningless lines and
no explanation of the *motif* or motive for the drawing can be
determined.

The distribution of the Lower Smithfield industries seems
to be very restricted. They are found in abundance in the
western part of the Orange Free State and the bordering regions
of the Cape Province, but not to any extent further westwards.
Southwards they are found as far as Craddock, but do not
appear beyond the mountains; eastwards they are perhaps
found as far as Smithfield, but not at all beyond, while northwards it is doubtful whether they can be traced further than
the Modder river. But, above all, Lower Smithfield settlements
are concentrated in the valley of the Riet from its junction with
the Modder eastwards. They are not found at all in Southern
Rhodesia. It would seem, then, that the Smithfield culture
must have been an autochthonous growth in South Africa itself,
probably developing somewhere near the Riet river[1].

The origin of the culture remains very obscure and is exceedingly puzzling. The concavo-convex side-scrapers above described are formed by a very specialised technique, and yet the
only other area where such objects are commonly found is in the
Nile valley and in the Fayum where they occur in pre-dynastic

---

[1] It is rather peculiar that in the Modder river valley Smithfield sites
are far less abundant than in the Riet river valley near by.

industries. They have also been noted in the industries found
in the Siwa oasis, which lies some 500 miles west of the Nile
and 200 miles south of the Mediterranean. But the absence
of all intervening links, such as would have been formed by the
finding of Lower Smithfield industries in Southern Rhodesia
and in other areas further north, are lacking. Are we to consider that these concavo-convex side-scrapers, with their special
technique, developed independently in South Africa, or are we
to consider that this technique was introduced from outside by
some folk who had learnt it long before from the pre-dynastic
people in the north, and whose culture was one of the elements
making up the Smithfield culture? The technique was used in
an area where indurated shale commonly occurs, for the flaking
of which material it is eminently suitable. The fine resolved
chipping found on the working edges of these tools perhaps
suggests that a still earlier Middle Palaeolithic element was
present in the composition of the new culture? It is quite possible to maintain the theory that a migration from the north,
subsequent to that which first brought Neoanthropic man
into South Africa, introduced a culture which interacted with
that of the Palaeolithic Fauresmith folk still living in what is
now the western part of the Orange Free State and the
adjacent districts of the Cape Province, the resulting hybrid
industry being partly determined by the fact that indurated
shale was the material close at hand for tool-making. Could
this foreign influence, modifying the older inhabitants, have
been the Wilton culture itself? At first sight the absence of
crescents in Smithfield industries, and of the other pigmy tools
so characteristic of the Wilton culture would argue against
this view. But crescents do occur occasionally, although it is
still uncertain whether they belong to the lower or upper
stage. The one we found in the Orange Free State (Fig. XVII,
15), which was typically Wilton in appearance, and the one
found by Mr Neville Jones at the same site have been already
mentioned. It may be objected that concavo-convex side-
scrapers are not found in Wilton industries, either in South
Africa or further north. The Wilton folk, however, were

essentially pigmy tool makers, i.e. their implements were composite (p. 90). Moreover, it was only where indurated shale, or fair-sized pieces of flinty material occurred, that the technique used in making the concavo-convex side-scrapers could be employed.

THE UPPER SMITHFIELD INDUSTRIES

A study of the Upper Smithfield industries reveals at once the fact that they are developed from those of the Lower Smithfield stage. " Duck-bills," indeed, occur in both; they are however generally more delicately made and show less patination in these industries of the later stage. But the really extraordinary thing is the immense quantities of them which now appear. In all sizes and shapes they litter the ground in thousands and literally barrow-loads of them can be collected in an afternoon (Fig. XVII, 7, 8, 9 and 17-22). The edges of the blade or flake are sometimes trimmed, sometimes not. Mr Van Riet Lowe has demonstrated the method probably used for their manufacture. He takes as an anvil a natural, flat, water-worn piece of indurated shale, such as can be found in any quantity close to a river margin. On this he lays a flake of indurated shale with its end just projecting over the edge; then with a trimming stone the working edge of the "duck-bill" is soon made and it is at once seen that by using this method the shoulders, already described in the case of Lower Smithfield "duck-bills," always develop between the working edge and the edges of the flake or blade. The freshness of the flaking of some of these "duck-bills" is a significant fact, and there is evidence to show that such tools were being manufactured by "Bush" folk up to only a very short time ago (50).

Fig. XVII. Smithfield industries. Round-scrapers, core-scrapers, portion of a stone ring (6), awls and crescent (15), a fragment of pottery (16), a European trade bead (24), duck-bills, and a knife-blade (23). From Modder river, Brakfontein, Klein Philippolis, near Queenstown, and Molteno. Note: Serrated edge on core-scraper (5): (15) is the first crescent found in the O.F.S.: (24) is thought to be not more than two hundred years old. All specimens made of indurated shale except 15, 16 and 24. Duck-bills are especially typical of Upper Smithfield industries.

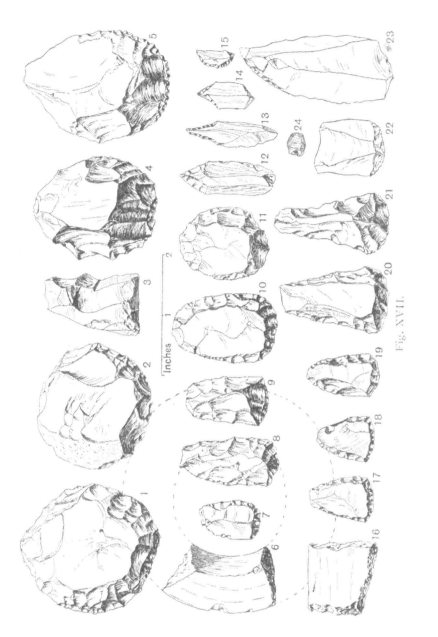

Fig. XVII.

Hollow scrapers, made on flakes and called by Mr Van Riet Lowe "spoke shaves," also occur. Trimming stones of all shapes, awls, points and the like are found in abundance. Bored stones (Fig. XVIII) as well as ostrich egg-shell beads, similar to those found in the Wilton culture, occur; a few bone awls or needles and a crude sort of pottery have also been found; we ourselves collected examples of the latter at Klein Philippolis. Ground and polished pestles consisting of rounded bars of indurated shale are also known (Fig. XVI, 8), as well as mortars which are simply slabs of shale or other suitable material slightly hollowed out. Although there is no evidence that Smithfield man practised agriculture or the domestication of animals, the presence of pestles and mortars or, more properly speaking, querns, together with pottery, rather argues that the culture should be assigned to a perhaps ill-developed, but definitely Neolithic civilisation (25). It must always be remembered that the Africa of Smithfield times must have teemed with game, making the domestication of animals unnecessary. In the same sort of way in East Anglia on the borders of the Fen country agriculture was not at all highly developed in Neolithic times, as is shown by the rarity of the sickle, an essential tool for the agriculturist. Doubtless these New Stone Age folk largely subsisted on game, which then abounded in the Fen country. Moreover a polishing technique—another feature of a Neolithic civilisation—at any rate for fashioning the working edges of tools is not unknown in Smithfield industries. Several examples have come from near Britstown[1].

At one or two sites, e.g. near Britstown by Mr Heese and at Riverton 20 miles or so north of Kimberley by Mr J. Power, a number of small double-shouldered points and fine needle-like

---

[1] These tools showing polish are very different, however, from the completely polished celt-like tool found at Battlefields in Southern Rhodesia, the affinities of which are not clearly understood, but which would seem to have some connection with similarly polished celts from the Congo. A portion of a polished specimen from Northern Rhodesia, now in the Museum of Archaeology and Ethnology at Cambridge, perhaps supplies an intervening link.

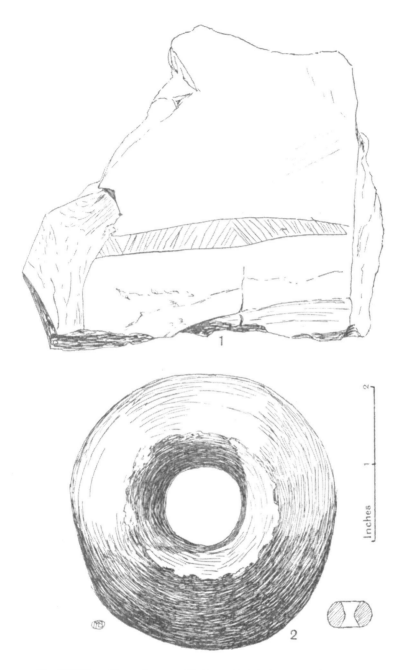

Fig. XVIII. 1. Piece of engraved indurated shale from De Kiel Oost, O.F.S.
2. Bored stone from site of new University buildings, Cape Town.

piercers showing trimming up both sides and recalling those found in pre-dynastic industries in the Fayum, etc. have been collected. May we not see here a strong Wilton influence? Mr Power has also found a beautiful tanged arrow-head, made from flinty material, in the floor of what was formerly a hut at Halfway House near Kimberley (p. 33). Tanged arrow-heads are exceedingly rare in South Africa. A few examples can be seen, however, in the Bloemfontein Museum and one in the South African Museum at Cape Town.

The distribution of the Upper Smithfield culture is somewhat wider than that of the Lower, and it is important to note that it is of common occurrence in painted rock-shelters in the mountain districts. In fact, as will be seen, it is to Upper Smithfield man that we owe all the well-known and beautiful polychromes and other paintings in the districts of Herschel, Aliwal North, Dordrecht, etc.

Upper Smithfield tools are also found in connection with the rock engravings, and they occur both at Vosberg and at Afvallingskop, as well as elsewhere[1].

Much controversy has been raised as to whether certain fragments of European bottleglass which are found on open Upper Smithfield sites are artefacts to be assigned to the Smithfield culture. We collected not a few such objects on the left bank just below the junction of the Modder and Riet rivers. Were they chipped by Upper Smithfield man? Dr Van Hoepen, who would like to ascribe the Smithfield culture to a very early date, claims that they are far more modern and that any chipping which can be observed on them is the result of the trampling over them of herds of animals. As a fragment of glass has in any case two parallel surfaces, nothing further is required to turn it into an effective scraping tool than a certain amount of trimming round the edges. It is therefore never likely that more than one direction of blow will be found, and the criterion necessary to prove that a piece of flint or other material had been fractured by man, viz. that there should be

[1] Mr Van Riet Lowe states that Lower Smithfield industries are also found with rock engravings.

evidence of blows in two or three definite directions, cannot
be expected. Personally I incline to the opinion that, although
in many cases Dr Van Hoepen is doubtless right, there are
examples preserved in the Kimberley Museum which, in all
probability, show human workmanship. As regards connection
with the Smithfield industry it would seem difficult in all
cases to dissociate these glass objects from the Smithfield tools,
and when we consider the extreme freshness visible on many of
the Upper Smithfield "duck-bills," there seems little reason to
consider that they are of any great antiquity and it is more
than probable that Upper Smithfield man continued to manufacture his industries even after the introduction of the glass
bottle by European traders.

The occurrence of trade beads of European manufacture in
Upper Smithfield industries seems to be fairly well authenti-
cated. This also argues for the modernity of the culture which
must have persisted until recent times.

THE KITCHEN MIDDEN INDUSTRIES (Fig. XIX)

All along the south-west, south and south-east coasts of the
Union, as well as to a certain distance inland, Kitchen Middens
have been found. They consist of immense heaps of the remains of shell fish which had formed the staple food of a sea-
board people. They are veritable rubbish heaps, but in them
have been discovered rich industries as well as skeletons. The
industries are not unlike those belonging to the Wilton culture,
lunates and small round scrapers having been found as well
as bored stones, bone awls, etc. Still in many ways it is more
convenient to class these industries as belonging to a separate
culture since the mode of life lived by the people themselves
must have been very different from that of the true Wilton
folk. This is shown by the fact that a number of special tools
suitable for such a sea-coast existence have been discovered.
It has been usual to describe the Kitchen Midden folk as
"strand-loopers" and to consider them as somewhat different
from the ordinary Bushman; but in all probability we should

rather talk of "strand-looping" than "strand-looper," and consider that we have to deal with a particular mode of life rather
than with a particular people. It would seem that for the most
part the "strand-loopers" were merely Bushmen who took to
the seashore (41) and that they were really allied to the folk
belonging to the Wilton culture.

A very good area for studying these Kitchen Middens is
just south of Port Elizabeth where they are found fringing
the coast for many miles. The enormous heaps, of varying
depth and of great extent, are a witness to the lengthy sojourn
there of these people. Besides some tools of Wilton type and
pottery there occur also sea-pebbles broken into halves and
smoothed down for use as pestles or grinders. In some instances
the smooth portion has a small rough hollow in the middle,
which is useful when grinding grain or other cereals (Fig.
XIX, 9). Large rough chopping tools also occur, made from sea-
pebbles (Fig. XIX, 10), and knives, awls and bored stones have
likewise been discovered.

The skeletons found are for the most part of Bushman or
Hottentot type, though Mr FitzSimons claims to have identi-
fied skeletons of a different, heavier build in the older layers
of Kitchen Midden material from some of the rock-shelters
near Zitzikama. This would confirm the theory that people of
more than one culture may have taken to a strand-looping
life (34) (35). One point of very great interest is the occurrence
of what are known as burial stones (Fig. XX). These consist of
large flat pebbles or fragments of broken mortars, often painted,
several of which were placed upon the body at burial. The
paintings sometimes depict rather conventionalised human
beings, sometimes animals and occasionally mere patterns in
colour. These finds forge another link between the Kitchen
Midden folk and the Wilton people, who, though they painted
no such burial stones themselves, were yet an artistic race who

---

Fig. XIX. Kitchen Midden industry showing a pot from the Ceres district, bone tools, Wilton-like pigmies from Still Bay, a pestle and a rough
chopping tool from near Port Elizabeth.

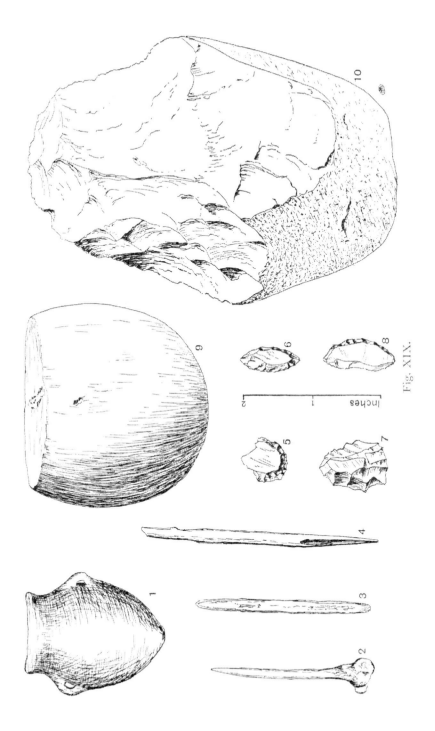

Fig. XIX.

inches

covered the walls of a large number of rock-shelters with paintings. Kitchen Midden material has also been found in many
rock-shelters, as, for example, near Fish Hoek, Hermanus,
Mossel Bay and Zitzikama (13)(14). In every case it forms the
most recent deposit in the rock-shelter. The industry contained is identical with that found in the ordinary Kitchen
Middens.

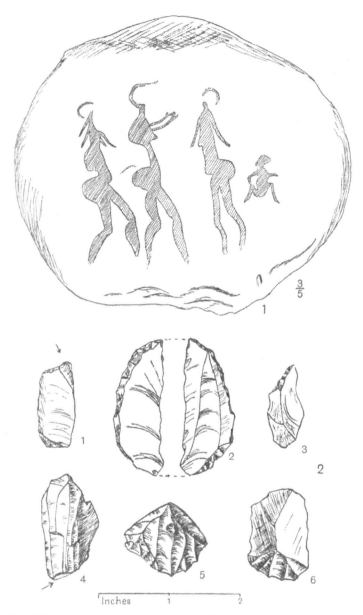

Fig. XX. 1. Painted burial stone, originally a portion or a mortar, from the Coldstream cave in the Mossel Bay district (after Péringuey). 2. Examples of the obsidian industry from Kenya, belonging to an Upper Palaeolithic culture.

CHAPTER VII

PREHISTORIC ART: GENERAL NOTIONS

ONE of the most fascinating branches of prehistoric study in South Africa is that of the art. Implements and weapons are essentially objects of everyday use and as such they are very helpful to the investigator in showing the kind of existence led by their primitive owners. But their study keeps us, as it were, in the kitchen or pantry, the toolhouse or the gunroom. We learn something of the prevailing mode of life, but nothing of the current ideas about, or outlook on, that life. Further, to some extent, outward conditions resulting from climate and the particular sort of material used for making the tools help to determine the appearance of an industry, and therefore from some points of view the industries are not merely the direct result of, and so are not completely indicative of, the *genius* of their makers. In the case of the art, however, this is not so. Even if motives of magic or ritual in some cases underlay its production, it is the result of an innate artistic tendency in the people, a something intensely personal and, as it were, extra and not essentially necessary to the actual business of living. Further, it is difficult to see how outside circumstances can have much modifying effect on its production. This is important, as there are paintings occurring as far north as eastern Spain which are exactly similar in style to those found at definite periods widely distributed in certain areas of South Africa—a strong argument for a connection between the parent cultures.

One often hears the term "Bushman paintings" used, but the expression has really very little meaning except in so far as the paintings are in many cases the work of various Bushman tribes. Not only are the multitudinous paintings and engravings known not all of the same age, but in addition, totally different styles of art exist in different geographical areas, and these different styles are sometimes found associated with different industries belonging to different cultures, as is proved by excavation in the soil of the painted rock-shelters themselves. The fact that investigations have to be made both from chronological and geographical points of view adds considerably to the complication of the problems for the student; but it is extremely important to keep these facts in mind, as quite a number of controversies have been started owing to investigators only knowing the art in their own area and apparently assuming that all Bushman art is the same art. Within the major geographical art groups, more especially among the paintings—for rock engravings, too, exist—we find it is possible to divide the figures into several series which had each perhaps a limited vogue in time, but a wide distribution in space. Sometimes paintings of a given series can be found in more than one geographical group, and such a phenomenon of course helps us to give a connected account of the art as a whole.

All the four methods of investigation that have been employed in studying the industries can be used in the study of the art, and, as before, stratigraphy and typology are the most important. Among both the rock engravings and the paintings it is often found that figures have been drawn one upon another, forming what in the case of ancient manuscripts would be called palimpsests. According to the law of superposition it follows that any drawing below must be older than one which is made above it. The difference in age may be small or great: perhaps only a few minutes, perhaps hundreds of years; but what is certain is that the lower drawing is the older of the two. The frontispiece shows an example of such a palimpsest which we studied at Makumbi. Further the various drawings are not all made in the same way with the same technique or in the same style—typologically as it were they are not all similar—and it has been found possible to determine a definite number of these different styles and techniques, both in the case of the engravings

and of the paintings. The important point is that when superpositions are studied it is found that the sequence of these
techniques and styles is always the same. Thus a chronological
order for the art groups can be obtained. In some cases the
different styles in an art group indicate, in all probability, an
evolution, or perhaps it might be better to say a fashion cycle,
all the styles being the work of the same people. In other cases
the changes in style are probably due to the arrival of other
allied tribes, doubtless belonging to the same stock though
actually differing in some ways from their predecessors.

Another factor which helps the modern investigator considerably in the study of the paintings is that, for reasons completely unknown and possibly merely capricious, the peoples
who drew in the various styles at different periods seem to
have preferred to use different colours, and thus we found in
the palimpsests, determined by stratigraphical considerations,
not only a sequence of styles, but actually a sequence of
colours; and over wide areas this colour sequence remained
constant. The question may well be asked: Why is this so? It
might be conceived that, coinciding with the change in style,
the artists of different periods at a given locality happened to
prefer different colours, the matter being of purely local importance. But why, then, this similar colour change over wide
areas? This question is by no means solved, and it involves
consideration of the possible motives for the art which will be
touched on in the sequel. It is sufficient for the moment to
state that the existence of colour and style sequences is obvious
to the investigator and is very helpful since it enables him to
assign, with fair probability, isolated drawings not in a palimp-
sest to a given series by noting their style and colour.

The last two methods of study, preservation and association,
are of less importance, although they have their uses locally.
Firstly with regard to the paintings, the action of weather is
most capricious and often the different parts of one panel are
not all similarly affected by it. Great care must therefore be
taken in deducing any information by this method. Caution
must also be exercised for another reason, namely that now

and then weathering action does, under certain circumstances, modify the colour of the original pigment. It is rare, however, if proper care is exercised, for this to be a disturbing factor in connection with colour sequences.

In the case of rock engravings the preservation method is distinctly more important. The engravings are found, for the most part, carved on dolerite rocks and boulders which patinate deeply but apparently comparatively slowly. Where then a figure is found, the engraved lines being patinated to the same depth and colour as the rock itself, where indeed the colour has become so similar that it is not always easy to distinguish the drawing, obviously a far greater antiquity can be postulated for the engraving in question than for those which are less or little patinated. It must be remembered that in the case of the engravings weathering action is a less capricious factor since they are generally all together in the open and completely exposed to the elements, being usually on the top of exposed kopjes. Thus what weathering there is affects the whole group at a given locality more or less similarly.

When considering the industries, "associations" refer to objects found with the tools, especially the remains of fauna. In the case of the art it is not the finding of an associated fauna that is helpful, but the study of the species of animals figured. For example, it would appear that among the engravings elephants are only figured in the earlier styles and techniques, probably because later they had disappeared from the particular district. A serious investigation into the question of the various species of animals figured in the different styles, requiring as it does a considerable knowledge of African fauna past and present, was, of course, out of the question for us who had but little or no knowledge of African animals, and too short a time at our disposal, but it is one worth attempting as a certain amount of information may accrue, of use not only to the prehistorian but also perhaps to the zoologist as well.

The colours used for the paintings were mostly derived from naturally occurring mineral oxides and iron carbonates which give, when powdered, various shades of red and yellow. Charcoal seems also to have been employed occasionally, although, as might be expected, this more fugitive pigment has not so well resisted the weathering action which goes on comparatively rapidly, even in such dry areas as South Africa and in rock-shelters which are to a certain extent protected from the wet. In one or two instances white paintings have been found. Where they are in granite country the white material, in all probability, is kaolin, which occurs in such regions as the weathered product of felspar. In other districts where I have seen white paint it struck me as having a very modern appearance, and it may well have been a preparation of wood ash, or even of *Euphorbia* latex, the poisonous milky sap which escapes when the bark of the *Euphorbia candelabra*, common in South Africa, is cut. One or two blue paintings are known in the Union. Here the pigment was probably obtained by powdering phosphatic nodules which could be found locally in shales.

In many cases the paintings are more or less waterproof, that is to say, with great care they can be washed and no colour will come off. This would seem to indicate that before it was applied to the rock wall the powdered material from which the paint was prepared was mixed with some medium which made it to a certain extent waterproof, and incidentally helped it to resist the weathering action to which it has been exposed. Such medium may have been made from gum or some other vege-table product. In this connection, too, Brother Otto, of the Mariannhill Monastery, suggests that the *Euphorbia* latex may have been used, which, if it is given time to harden, forms a sort of waterproof skin, thus rendering the paintings impervious to anything but mechanical weathering. Even the mixing of the powdered coloured material with animal fat would yield a fairly firm permanent paint, and it is quite possible that in many cases this was the method employed. How the colour was applied is unknown, but some of the techniques of making the figures in the various styles will be noted in due course.

As has been said, both paintings and engravings occur. These will be described separately, for, unfortunately, as yet, no instance has been found where both occur together as a palimp-sest; and so, although we are able to offer a chronological sequence for each, it has not yet been found possible to correlate the two sequences together. Perhaps in some such area as Bechuanaland paintings and engravings will be found in superposition one with another and it will then be possible.

CHAPTER VIII

PREHISTORIC ART: SOUTHERN RHODESIA

BY far the best area in which to start an investigation of rock-shelter paintings is Southern Rhodesia. This is partly owing to the fact that the country is but sparsely occupied by white men, and that, until recently at any rate, the native has tended to shun the painted localities, treating them as sacred spots not to be interfered with. In consequence they are frequently well preserved, though unfortunately now, as has been the case in the Union when painted localities are situated near towns, they sometimes become a resort for picnic parties whose favourite occupation seems to be that of throwing stones at the paintings, thus destroying them utterly, or of drawing outlines round the figures in white chalk which is very nearly as bad. The passion for destruction on the one hand, and for inscribing one's name or making other marks on the other, is, however, as old as humanity and little can be done to eradicate it. There is, therefore, all the more reason that investigation should be speedily undertaken, so that precious information may be obtained before it is too late. Another reason why Southern Rhodesia seems to me to be a specially favoured area is because the migrations into South Africa must have passed through this country in their southward trek, and so we are likely to find here a fairly complete series of their works. Also the migrations would tend to be focussed in this region; the Zambesi must have been crossed either above the gorge which starts at the Victoria Falls, or just below it, but probably not anywhere much further to the east as the country and the crossing would then be of considerable difficulty. It is true the Pongwe flats are open country, but they are a low-lying area frequently flooded, and the river itself, even in summer, must have formed a difficult barrier to negotiate.

PLATE IV

Painted panel at Nswatugi, Matopos.

The Beatrice Road site near Salisbury, S. Rhodesia.

ART: SOUTHERN RHODESIA

Road site (Plate IV), is to be found 7 miles from Salisbury and
half a mile to the right of the Hunyani Road on the further
side of a small river. It is granite country and a number of
isolated kopjes half-covered with a straggly bush growth can
be seen scattered around. Half-way up one of these small kopjes
is a large granite boulder wedged in a small rock-shelter not
unlike a dentist's gag in the mouth of his victim. This boulder
or wedge has been covered with paintings, there being also
some nearly weathered away examples on the ceiling of the
rock-shelter itself. Actually at the site no "home" exists and
no implements of any kind have been found, but on the other
side of the kopje at its base there appears to have been a small
settlement. The painted boulder faces nearly east. Standing
by its side one enjoys a magnificent view. To get close up to
the paintings is a matter of considerable difficulty. There is
only a narrow ledge in front of them, and to reach this ledge
one has to wriggle serpent-wise along a narrow fissure for some
yards, there being a nasty drop on to rocks and scrub on the
left-hand side.

An examination of the main panel shows that the following
colours are present:

Dark claret, dark brownish-red, orange-yellow and bright
red.

A number of superpositions occur yielding the following
information:

Orange-yellow was painted over bright red and is therefore
the more recent.

Dark claret was painted over dark brownish-red and is
therefore the more recent.

Dark brownish-red is painted over orange-yellow and is
therefore the more recent.

From these facts there results the following sequence:

Dark claret—most recent.
Dark brownish-red.
Orange-yellow   ⎫ Very similar in style and probably
Bright red—the earliest⎭ not very different in age.

The bright red series includes drawings of horses and one of the typical forms of representation of a human being, that is to say a figure with body horizontal, more or less "on all fours." In the orange-yellow series there are also some poorly drawn men. In the dark brownish-red series elephant and buck are depicted and the dark claret series includes drawings of buffalo, sable antelope and men. There were also figures of an older series that had been altered by the artists using dark claret and redrawn in the new colour. A noticeable factor, too, was the occurrence of areas of dashes arranged in a flowing sort of formation. These probably represent water, either in the form of rain or a stream. The latter perhaps is the more likely, as in one case the lines of dashes were crossed by two parallel lines possibly meant to represent a bridge[1]. As might be expected, the dark claret coloured dashes composing this sort of stream often occur in contact with figures in other colours belonging to the other series; they are always drawn over them, definitely confirming the fact that the dark claret series is the most recent one here present[2].

Two other very important sites occur 20 miles north of Salisbury in the Chindamora Native Reserve; one at Domboshawa and the other 12 miles further on in the Mawanga Hills, called Makumbi.

The site at Domboshawa (Plate V) consists of a large main rock-shelter between two subsidiary sites found a short distance to the right and to the left. The main cave opens to the east, and down in the valley below water can readily be obtained. The colours seen were black, dark claret, bright red and orange. Superpositions showed that in this case the orange was apparently the most ancient of all the colours present, for it is covered in two instances by red figures, and that, as always, dark claret paintings are clearly seen on the top of bright red figures. In this site no dark brownish-red paintings were seen.

[1] Compare the "rain god" at Domboshawa (p. 119).
[2] The investigator must be careful at this particular site because the dark claret series tends to weather to a colour not dissimilar to the earlier dark brownish-red. The style of the drawings, however, is different.

PLATE V

Domboshawa near Salisbury: general view and paintings.

In the orange-yellow series there are several—and formerly, before their destruction by picnic parties, there were many more—splendidly drawn paintings of koodoo. A rhinoceros and some human beings are also figured. In the bright red series too some men are depicted. Among these there are a number whose bodies and limbs are elongated to such an enormous extent that "daddy-long-legs" is the only name which describes them. There are also some well-drawn animals, sometimes filled in with colour, sometimes only outlined. In the dark claret series the colour is matt and not glossy as it is in some sites; the figures are not so well drawn as in the earlier styles, but buffalo and elephant are depicted. The black drawings include small men carrying spears, they are isolated from the rest of the figures, have a fresh appearance, and are certainly by far the most recent in date. They are but few in number.

To the left of the main shelter, under an overhanging rock, some men attacking an elephant with tusks are painted in dark claret. On the same wall are some figures of men with bows painted in black, the style being almost spider-like as if the drawings had been made with a pen. Although there is no superposition, these figures are probably later in age than the elephant group just described. There is also an excellent drawing in dark claret of a quadruped which is possibly a zebra or a quagga. Lastly there are the figures of a man and animal painted in red.

To the right of the main rock-shelter is one of the most interesting paintings that we came across. It was discovered by Mr Goodwin when prowling about while we were tracing some of the other drawings, and I fancy that it had not been previously noted as it was completely new to Mr Broderick, of the Government Native Industrial School close by, who was most kindly conducting our party on this occasion. The scene represents a human being apparently pouring out rain, depicted by a number of dashes, over what must be meant to represent a tree. The whole belongs to the dark claret series in which colour it is painted. A tradition exists among the local Bantu natives to-day which connects this cave at Domboshawa with

the production of rain. In fact the place is really a sacred spot
and, until recently, in times of drought pilgrimage was made
there to obtain rain. The method of procedure was to bring
offerings to the cave and wait there for some time until the
sign that the offerings had been accepted and therefore that
rain would come appeared. The sign took the form of smoke
issuing from the top of the great round granite dome of the
hill itself, in the side of which the rock-shelter opens. The
mechanics of the phenomenon would seem to have been due to
the following circumstances. At the back of the rock-shelter
are the beginnings of a huge fissure which apparently continues
through the rock right away to the top of the hill, forming, as
it were, a sort of chimney. Under certain conditions the smoke
from a fire lit in the cave would be drawn up this fissure or
chimney and would issue out at the top of the mountain.
This would only take place when the wind was blowing from
a particular direction, i.e. from the east whence rain normally
came. This explains why the suppliants often had to wait a
considerable time before their requests were granted, even when
all the necessary ritual performances had duly taken place.
They had to wait, indeed, till the wind went round to draw the
smoke up to the top of the mountain, and, incidentally, to bring
up the clouds.

But the dark claret series to which the drawing of the "rain-
god" belongs is undoubtedly far older than the Bantu period
and this interesting method of rain-production, and it would
seem that we have here an instance of a new people taking
over the traditions, and perhaps practices, of the folk into whose
country they had penetrated. A good example of such a continued reverence for and utilisation of spots already sanctified
can be seen in the building of Christian churches on the top of
tumuli and other spots which had been sacred in pre-Christian
days. In some cases the motive behind this continuation of
traditions may have been one of fear: a desire to appease or
counteract the powers of evil by placing on them an embargo
of the new and stronger cults. But more often it would seem
that the newcomers took over the existing popular beliefs with

but little change; just as in Christian times the pagan spirit of the spring or of the cliff was incorporated into the terminology of the mediaeval church in France, and we find as a result such dedicatory names as *Notre Dame de la Fontaine,* or *Notre Dame de la Falaise.* Domboshawa was probably a sacred spot connected with rain production from very ancient times and its sacredness continued even through the change of the dominant culture in the neighbourhood. South Africa is a dry land; whoever they may have been, who in past times invaded and occupied the country, they must very soon have found that their thoughts and desires centred round the necessity for water, which is there of paramount importance, though its lack seldom troubles us here in England and is therefore hard for us to appreciate.

Makumbi, whither Mr Broderick most kindly led us over very difficult country (Plate 1), is an immense cave about 100 yards long by 30 yards deep; it faces north-east and is situated high up in the top of a magnificent rounded granite hill. So steep and smooth is the rock surface of the hill that one has to climb round the side of it, preferably with rubber-soled shoes or with stockinged feet. No water is to be found nearer than the bottom of the hill; it actually only takes about 15 minutes to get down to it, but a much longer time to get up again. Most of the back wall of the shelter and part of the ceiling, especially towards the back where it is very low, is literally covered with paintings and the mere number of them is astounding. In the shallow soil of the rock-shelter an industry occurs, but no very good or very definite tools were unearthed, though many quartz flakes, etc. and pottery of various ages were found.

The following colours were noted:

Yellow, earthy-yellow, dark claret, dark reddish-brown, white, red and black. Superpositions yielded the following information:

Black	Dark claret	Dark reddish-brown
Red	Dark reddish-brown	Yellow
Dark reddish-brown	Earthy-yellow	Earthy-yellow
Red	Yellow	Dark claret
White	White	White
Dark claret	Red	Dark reddish-brown

The order of age is therefore:

Black ⎫ Probably in this order of sequence though
White ⎬ not definitely shown by superpositions.
Earthy yellow ⎭
Dark claret.
Dark reddish-brown.
Yellow ⎫ These two are clearly the oldest but their relative
Red ⎭ age could not be determined[1].

Paintings of the black series are very rare, there being only a sign composed of a circle enclosing a heart-shaped figure. In the white series there are paintings of an elephant and rhinoceros (poorly drawn) and two immense figures, 6 feet or more in length, possibly meant to represent hanging skins or perhaps shields. In the earthy-yellow series buck can be noted and some meandering lines, while in the dark claret series we find men and buck, including an attractive koodoo (Frontispiece), all fairly well drawn, and occasionally figures executed in what can best be described as a "stippling" technique quite unlike the usual paintings which are generally in uniform colour. In the dark reddish-brown series elephant, buck and buffalo were observed. Some of the paintings consisted of large outlined figures well drawn. In the yellow series buck only were noted, but in the red series as well as buck and men there were paintings in outline, one of which depicted a zebra, its stripes indicated by parallel bars across the body and legs. Specially notable, too, was a large red figure of a man 1 ft. 5 in. in length. It occurs, together with other rather similar figures, in a frieze on the roof. Bunches of what might fancifully be taken for leaves were also found in the red series and somewhat similar figures have been noted at Domboshawa painted in the same colour. This summary of the paintings noted does not in any way pretend to be complete. In the short time at our disposal we could only make notes of, and can here only indicate, what appeared to be the most important features. It was heartrending not to be able to spend a fortnight at this most fascinating place. It would be well worth while for an expedition of picked investigators to study carefully

[1] In this connection see Beatrice Road site and Domboshawa.

and publish an account of the art which is still to be found there; more especially so as, since the site is hidden away deep in the Native Reserve, it has not yet been discovered by chance tourists, and I am happy to say that I saw no single modern name desecrating the walls.

Near Salisbury other similar painted localities of lesser importance are to be found; among these we visited the Quarry site a mile or two south of the town, and another on Mr Phear's farm, and still another close to the homestead of the M. T. C. farm, about 5 miles south-east of the town. These are smaller rock-shelters and not so striking as the ones described above, but at the last named a similar sequence of colours can be noted, earthy-yellow being the most modern, then dark claret, then dark red or reddish-brown, and finally light red as the earliest. Apparently the yellow series is missing here. At the M. T. C. site figures of the earthy-yellow series are sometimes partly outlined in red and are, I fancy, to be connected in style with what we found in a cave in the Matopos, called Nswatugi (Plate IV), where tentative attempts at polychrome painting can be seen. The relative age of this earthy-yellow series is quite clear, as it occurs in superposition above an animal painted in dark claret. In the dark claret series there is an interesting zebra-like animal painted in stripes; weathering has slightly worn away the rock between the stripes where it is unprotected by the paint, almost giving an appearance of slight relief. Besides the zebra there is an elephant painted in dark claret. In the dark red series we find koodoo, and in the light red series men. The ground was much overgrown with grass and bushes and so we collected no tools there, indeed it does not seem likely that any settlement could have existed just where the paintings are as there was not a very suitable rock-shelter.

Another group of interesting painted sites is found in the Matopo Hills in that extraordinarily fascinating granite country near Bulawayo, where huge boulders are piled on other boulders as if giants of long ago had been playing with bricks upon a gigantic nursery floor and, growing tired, had petulantly left them in a glorious confusion. Since then a bushy growth, miraculously finding existence possible among the nooks and crannies of the rocks, has in some measure softened the hard and somewhat callous effect which the giants' untidiness gave to the countryside.

A number of hemispherical rock-shelters occur among the granite boulders. They are due to natural weathering action, and although but very few have, as yet, been examined from the prehistorian's point of view, several of them have been found to be painted sites, and not infrequently rich industries have been excavated from the floors of the shelters. Visitors to the "World's View" are sometimes shown two small bushman painted sites, the first known as the "Bushman Cave" and the second as "Pomongwe." Neither of these, however, are of any very great scientific interest, and at the latter the paintings have been somewhat damaged by an attempt to brighten them by dabbing on some oily or glycerine-like substance. In the "Bushman Cave" three different series of paintings can be distinguished, the earliest being in red, the next in glossy white and the latest—obviously modern, probably Matabele—in chalky white, and very inferior in drawing. Reference to the more complete sequence at Makumbi already given in this chapter will at once indicate what series are missing. The styles of the earlier two series of paintings perfectly agree with the corresponding ones of the Makumbi sequence.

A more important site is to be found about 3½ miles along a footpath over the hills from Whitewater, a small Mission out-station on the Antelope Mine Road some 40 miles or more from Bulawayo and beyond the railway terminus of the Matopo branch line. The name of the place is Nswatugi (Plate IV), and the hill from which the "World's View" is obtained lies perhaps 12 miles or so away "as the crow flies." The cave itself (33) opens nearly at the end of a steep gully—at its entrance it measures about 6 yards across and has a maximum depth of some 15 yards. It was at once obvious that, as at Salisbury, a sequence of styles could be readily determined, each different style being as before painted in a different colour and corresponding to the styles found round Salisbury.

The superpositions were as follows:

$$\frac{\text{Earthy-yellow}}{\text{White}} \qquad \frac{\text{Polychrome}}{\text{White}} \qquad \frac{\text{Polychrome}}{\text{Dark brownish-red}}$$

$$\frac{\text{Figures whose bodies are filled in with lines}}{\text{Dark brownish-red}}$$

$$\frac{\text{White}}{\text{Dark claret}} \qquad \frac{\text{Dark claret}}{\text{Dark brownish-red}}$$

$$\frac{\text{Dark claret}}{\text{Figures whose bodies are filled in with lines}}$$

and also

$$\frac{\text{A large area of dots}}{\text{Dark brownish-red}}$$

These give us the following sequence:

Polychrome ⎫ Probably to be closely connected together and very
Earthy-yellow ⎭ similar in age [1].

White ⎰ In one instance associated with dark claret and therefore not far
⎱ distant from it in age.

Dark claret.

Figures whose bodies ⎫
are filled in with ⎬ In one case associated with dark claret and
lines ⎭ therefore not far distant from it in age.

Dark brownish-red—Earliest here found.

In the polychrome series there are some beautiful giraffe, zebra, human figures and signs.

In the white series: a "rain bull" (?).

In the dark claret series: men, etc.

In the "filled in with lines" series: giraffe and elephant.

In the dark brownish-red series: koodoo and human beings of both sexes.

The Nswatugi cave is thus seen to be extremely interesting. The sequence of the styles, as also of colours, agrees with what we have hitherto found, but it seems that the various series here grade into one another and are less sharply distinct than has been the case elsewhere. For example, the "filled in with lines" series is very distinct from the white series, but in between is found the dark claret series which in its latest phase is

[1] In this connection see p. 123.

associated with the white series and in its earlier phase with an elephant belonging to the "filled in with lines" series. The complete absence of the earlier yellow and bright red series may also be noted as interesting. Can we connect this circumstance with the fact that on excavating the floor of the rockshelter only a Wilton industry has been found, whereas at another cave not far off, called Bambata, where paintings of the bright red series are present, not only is a Wilton industry found in the cave but, stratigraphically below it, an industry belonging to another culture very different indeed from the Wilton, a culture which, as suggested in Chapter V, may in fact have been left by an earlier Neoanthropic migration into South Africa? The occurrence of polychrome paintings at Nswatugi is also a matter of special interest in view of the fact that they form the latest series of the sequence. Further south in the Union a polychrome technique is frequently employed, the drawings being, however, far more developed and the various colours used in many different ways. At Nswatugi we seem to see the tentative beginnings of polychrome work before the artist had quite realised the possibilities of the new method. One or two of the polychrome figures of humans painted in red, yellow and white are of special interest as they resemble the figures lately found in a cave not far from Fort Victoria which Dr Impey considers to be pictures of very early Egyptians.

This interesting site, which Colonel Carbutt with special kindness took us to visit, is on Dr Williams' farm "Iram" (p. 36). The painted site is reached by continuing 7 miles beyond the homestead of this farm over a practically trackless region of low bush. Then where the ground begins to fall rapidly, and there is a glorious view over wild hill and dale, there rises an isolated kopje, near one end of which, a little way up from its base, opens the low rock-shelter in question, which we have ventured to name after Dr Impey, "Impey's Cave" (Plate II). On the floor of the shelter there is an immense rounded boulder which clearly must at some time have fallen from directly above, leaving a gap of only 3 ft. 6 in. between its upper surface and the present low curved roof. It is on this roof that the famous painted panel

occurs, and as may be imagined anything in the nature of photo-
graphy, or even tracing, is a matter of considerable difficulty.
The panel is very small—it could be contained in a rectangle
measuring 2¼ ft. by 1½ ft. It consists of a number of human
figures in some cases bearing in their hands what might seem
to be musical instruments[1]. They are painted in polychrome
and are not unlike some of those at Nswatugi.

The colours seen are pink (produced by painting in white
over dark claret), white and brownish-yellow. The style of the
figures is very difficult to describe; the bodies are not filled in
with uniform flat colour, but with several colours, there being
definite lines of demarcation between them. This has given rise
in Dr Impey's mind to the conjecture that clothes are meant
to be indicated, and he considers that the types of clothing
depicted are exactly similar to those worn by the very early
Egyptians. He further believes that the panel represents a scene
of music and dancing. On these grounds he rejects the Bushman
origin for this and much of the rock-shelter art in South Africa
and suggests that it was the work of some far earlier people.

Let us look again at the panel itself; a careful examination
shows that a figure of a man to the left of the group is clearly
drawn over a much decayed painting of a sessabi in the dark
claret style and colour, and that further, detached from the
group, we have a dark claret sign painted over a reddish-brown
animal. Clearly then the polychrome group is the most modern
of all the paintings in this shelter. It belongs, in my opinion,
to the same series as the polychromes of Nswatugi, in fact, to
the last series of Southern Rhodesian paintings.

For many reasons it is difficult to imagine that these paint-

---

[1] These did not, however, seem to us to be always quite as Dr Impey
has reproduced them. For instance, he shows one figure holding a long
white flute-like instrument in his two hands. But on a close examination
the surface of the granite is seen to be covered with irregular white
speckles, probably small felspar crystals, and with a little imagination it
is quite easy to persuade oneself that the lines into which these resolve
themselves are really lines of white paint. We could not convince ourselves that the flute had ever been painted. This, of course, was by no
means invariably the case and undoubtedly in many instances the figures
are carrying interesting objects in their hands.

ings were actually drawn by Egyptians themselves in predynastic or early dynastic times. It is possible, however, that the influence of Egyptian culture may have continued to be felt among the various peoples who were slowly making their way southwards through the continent long after it had ceased to be important in the land of its origin. This point has already been touched on in connection with the Smithfield industry, the distribution of which shows clear indication that it was a wholly South African development, though the industries include types of tools strongly recalling similar types found in Egypt at Badari and in the Fayum. It did not seem to us that all the claims made by Dr Impey as to types of clothes, musical instruments, and the suggestion that the people in the group were perhaps a school of dancing or music or even deportment, could be substantiated; but undoubtedly the panel is of very considerable interest. As we have said, however, the style of the paintings is not unique.

Higher up the kopje, above the cave, there are a number of large complicated rock-shelters which seem to have been inhabited by the Mashona people at a comparatively recent date, probably at the time of the first coming of the Matabele into the country. Any quantity of what appears to be ordinary typical Mashona pottery can be collected, and, though much broken, complete vessels can easily be reconstructed out of the fragments.

A small but exceedingly delightful painted panel occurs in a place called Kempsie Glen on Mr Readman's farm, off the 'Ndanga Road, not far from Fort Victoria. To get to it the farm "Niekerksrust" must first be reached. From there three kopjes are seen on the right hand and the site in question is half-way up the middle one. The paintings (Fig. XXI) are quite exposed on a small rock surface which faces the setting sun. Though few in number they are well drawn and represent three couples—two pairs of koodoo, and a man and woman hand in hand. One pair of koodoo and the human beings are painted in dark brownish-red, the other pair of koodoo in dark claret. From a consideration of style, coupled with the evidence obtained

Fig. XXI. Paintings of koodoo and humans from Readman's Farm near Fort Victoria, S. Rhodesia. The pair to the right are painted in dark claret; the other figures are in dark brownish-red. Scale about ¼ nat. size.

from localities already described, the two couples in brownish-red probably belong to an earlier series than the couple in dark claret, though no superpositions actually occur. In the case of the dark claret figures there is clear evidence to show that a careful outline was first drawn and that the whole bodies were then filled in with colour. It is possible that the same is true of the earlier series, but it was less apparent. The male koodoo of both the couples has delightful long wavy horns and a beard. The place itself can hardly have been a "home" site, although there are plenty of rock-shelters suitable for habitation in the vicinity. It was evening when we visited it and as the sun sank down in the west below us, flooding the panel with golden light, there was something inexpressibly gracious in this small and almost unknown scene, with the two little people hand-in-hand in the middle and the two pairs of koodoo, one nibbling the branch of a tree. Lower down on the same kopje in a small rock-shelter the figure of an ostrich painted in dark claret was discovered. Scaling of the rock surface had removed the colour from the middle part of the body. Formerly it must have been a fine drawing of considerable size measuring about 10 in. by 6 in.

About 11 miles on the other side of Fort Victoria, that is to the north-west, lies the Jesuit Mission at Gokomere. Father Gardner, who is stationed there, has explored the district with great energy, and has excavated a typical Wilton industry in quartz from below a large rock-shelter close to the Mission House itself. All round under the granite boulders of the kopjes are innumerable rock-shelters, a great many of which show the remains, at any rate, of painted panels. Only two styles and colours were noted, viz. the dark claret and the earthy-yellow, and in one instance at least a superposition showed that the former was, as usual, the earlier in age. At Gokomere then we have no examples of the earlier series of the paintings of the country. With the exception perhaps of a queer inexplicable figure in dark claret, associated with lines and dots, which may have had some symbolic meaning, there was nothing further of special interest.

It is now appropriate to summarise the conclusions arrived at as the result of our work in Southern Rhodesia. Notably our investigations indicated clearly the existence of several art series of different ages. First and oldest, we have a number of red or yellow paintings nicely drawn, usually in uniform flat colour, though occasionally in outline only. Next we have a slightly more modern series in dark brownish-red (varying locally from dark red to dark brown), the style of which, although perhaps more developed, still recalls the earlier series with which therefore it may be considered to have some connection. Then appears the dark claret series which is quite different from anything that has come before, both in colour and in style. There is a certain angularity about these drawings that has not been hitherto apparent—something rather Japanese in appearance, although, of course, the style is still completely naturalistic. The paintings have clean sharp outlines, curves and angles of horns, and bodies are well and finely drawn; their style is vigorous and attractive, and one feels that a fine point must have been used in their production and that often the outlines must have been drawn first and the whole figure filled in carefully later. This series very definitely divides those which precede it from those which follow. Lastly, we have several series, earthy-yellow, white and the beginnings of polychrome, which can be definitely classed together as later than the dark claret series. The paintings of these groups show quite a different style of art; the polychromes are of course unmistakable, but even with the other colours the style is very distinctive and much less attractive. The animal figures are heavier and their bodies less shapely and their legs stiffer. I fancy the few examples in black that we noted are the latest drawings of all and may be neglected for our purposes as being comparatively modern, possibly of Bantu origin. This makes altogether five different age periods that can with safety be determined, but it is perhaps simpler to think in terms of three groups: an early pre-dark claret one, a middle one composed only of the dark claret series and a later one including the earthy-yellow and white series and apparently leading up to and consummated in the polychrome series.

In studying this art it must be remembered that it is a fortuitous though helpful circumstance that we can get so much information from colour sequences, but that too much reliance should not be placed on colour alone, as it is differences of style that really count. Colours, too, are naturally not quite constant, for instance at Makumbi those of the dark brownish-red and dark claret series approach each other closely[1]. But the observer who has carefully looked at the various paintings in several sites will probably find it far easier to recognise the different styles than to explain their differences. Unfortunately the reader may not be able to distinguish the differences of style very well from the few illustrations in this book, for although they are reduced from actual tracings it is not only the outline which contributes to the style of the painting, but also the effect of the *tout ensemble*—the painting in its own setting with its own rock background. Moreover, with the best intentions in the world, it is hard for the tracer not to contribute something of his own to the work, more especially in places where the paintings are faint or decayed, and this must to some extent tend to give an intangible common factor to all the art traced and copied by the same hand.

[1] The dark claret series have a more glossy appearance.

CHAPTER IX

PREHISTORIC ART: CENTRAL AND SOUTHERN GROUPS

PAINTINGS OF THE CENTRAL GROUP

IT was a great regret to us that circumstances prohibited a visit to any of the painted sites which are known to occur in the north-eastern Transvaal. It would have been interesting to have known how far south the various series of the Rhodesian sequence penetrated, and whether a similar sequence could have been determined, for instance, in the case of the paintings near Barberton or around Lake Chrissie. Again, although no examples of art have hitherto been recorded, it would have been interesting, had time permitted, to have explored some of the hill ranges in the northern Transvaal. However, this could not be accomplished and the next painted cave that we were able to study was in a rock-shelter in the hillside above the Mission House at Modderpoort. Modderpoort is on the railway line from Bloemfontein to Natal, in the Orange Free State province of the Union, and it was interesting to contrast the art there with that of Rhodesia with which we had become so familiar. Here paintings of the special type occur, which is found in many sites fringing the mountainous backbone of the Union. Such paintings are especially well exemplified in rock-shelters in the National Park on the Natal side of the Drakensberg, and also in Basutoland and in the districts of Herschel, Aliwal North, etc. The physical nature of the ground is eminently suitable for rock-shelter art, for the local rock is of the type known as cave sandstone. This deposit weathers unevenly and so literally thousands of rock-shelters are formed which can be seen in bands along the side of the hills, wherever there are outcrops of the sandstone.

A distinguishing feature of this art group is the large number of beautifully painted polychrome figures of animals. The various colours seem to have been applied separately, there being a definite line of demarcation between them. In only a few instances did we find them shading into one another, as would have been the case if the artist had rubbed or brushed over the hard dividing line and so merged one colour with its neighbour. The forequarters and under parts of an animal are generally depicted in white, the body being most usually painted in yellow ochre, with sometimes here and there a touch of brick red or dark claret. The horns are often black. Human beings, too, are painted in more than one colour and the frequent elongation of the human form, which makes the bodies look as if they had been pulled out on the rack, is noteworthy. At many places in this geographical area of the hill country one can see the remains of painted figures which appear to belong to the dark claret series of Southern Rhodesia. These figures however give one the impression that the art of this series is here in a more developed stage than it was in Southern Rhodesia. Where overlapping occurs they are found below the polychrome paintings we have just described. The polychromes themselves show signs of evolution from simple forms, somewhat similar to those we saw in Southern Rhodesia, rising to a wonderful level of artistic merit and then degenerating to harder, more angular, less pleasing figure drawing. It is, of course, the uppermost figures of this series which show a distinct falling off in execution and beauty. Frequently when figures in black occur they are the most modern of all.

It is notable and significant that whenever industries have been found associated with paintings of this art group they can be referred to the Upper Smithfield culture[1].

To return to Modderpoort (48); the site itself is of especial interest from many points of view. On entering the rock-shelter the visitor is at once confronted by a magnificent polychrome panel in the centre of which are two animals, evidently buck head-to-head. The colours of these polychromes are dark red, yellow, white, dark claret and black. They are themselves painted over dark claret figures which show a series of white lines

---

[1] But see p. 100.

depending from their outstretched arms[1]. Two steatopygous figures of men, also painted in dark claret, can be seen lower down to the right of the polychrome panel. Elsewhere in the rock-shelter there is a dichrome group of elongated men painted in dark claret and black, or in black alone. In one instance there is a dark claret figure whose shadow is carefully drawn in black. In another part of the rock-shelter is a little human figure carrying a digging stick weighted with a bored stone, and on the ceiling to the right is what is evidently a battle scene, with the figures painted in black. Below this, two animals are figured in dark claret, one is headless but has the long curled-up tail typical of a lion. Elsewhere we noted a baboon, a man on "all fours," buck and what may have been finger prints consisting of black dots enclosed in an earthy brown ring. Near by there were also some dark claret punctuations. At Nolan's Kloof, less than 10 minutes' easy walk from Van Reenan station at the top of the famous pass from Natal into the Free State and not so very far from Modderpoort, there is another site where polychrome paintings very similar to those we have just described can be seen. They are typical of the art found on the sites that fringe the mountain massif.

Further south, in the districts round Molteno and Dordrecht we were touching the classic country, the art of which was described and copied by Stow and in part also most ably published by Miss Helen Tongue (48). Numberless sites have been discovered all over this district from Aliwal North on the one hand to Sterkstroom on the other. In no case did we observe any paintings that would be classed as belonging to anything earlier than the middle or dark claret series if they had been found in Rhodesia. Indeed the earliest paintings recognised, while they compare in colour and style with the Rhodesian middle series, yet seem to be more developed and therefore more modern than their counterparts in the north. Polychromes on the other hand abound and are sometimes of extreme beauty. Some time ago a fine example of a polychrome

[1] Compare Tylden, p. 139.

group fell from the roof of the rock-shelter at Zaamen Komst Farm, 12 miles from Maclear, and has been removed to the South African Museum at Capetown. It has been reproduced in colour in the *Transactions of the Royal Society of South Africa* for 1927. The paintings are as fine as anything which could, under the same circumstances, be made to-day. They show a herd of elands with bodies shaded from white to yellow or sometimes very dark red, with white heads, necks and limbs. The animals are all trotting, or rather being driven, from left to right.

At Kilgobbin Farm, near Molteno, there are some most interesting paintings depicting white men on horseback wearing the large wide-brimmed hats of the veldt farmer. It is amusing to note that the peculiar turned up sides of the brims of these hats have caught the artist's eye for in each case they are saliently portrayed. The style of the paintings, which have degenerated since the best polychrome days, is very inferior indeed. The figures are stiff, square and wooden and lack a sense of grace or movement. A number of superpositions of various colours were noticed, but the drawings did not differ from one another to any great extent in style. I am inclined to think that while, as must necessarily be the case, prehistorians are engaged with the broad outline of South African prehistory rather than with the smaller local details, it can safely be assumed that throughout this region the paintings almost all belong more or less to one decidedly modern series. There are, on the one hand, traces of an earlier series perhaps connected with the later ones of Southern Rhodesia, and on the other hand there is a steady degeneration of the polychromes of which the latest examples are quite inferior drawings.

Several miles from Molteno, in a gorge on the right bank of a little running stream about a quarter of a mile to the left of the road from Molteno to Kilgobbin, there is another notable site. It contains an interesting panel depicting what is no doubt a hunting scene. Bantus with red earrings and metal spears, and also a dead animal, are portrayed. This panel is clearly

Fig. XXII. 1. Purplish painting of an elephant in a krantz opposite Dordrecht. 2. Fine black figure of an ostrich in a painted krantz about 9 miles from Tarkastad.

the latest of a series at that locality, and superpositions showed
the order of the colours to be as follows:

The Bantu scene ...	Most modern.
A red series	Perfectly different in style from and not to be correlated with the bright red series of Southern Rhodesia.
An earthy-yellow series	
A dark claret series ...	Oldest.

At this rock-shelter there occurred a rich Smithfield industry,
and further up the gorge we found what had probably been a
Smithfield factory site.

On the other side of Molteno, 6 miles from the town and to
the left of the Tarkastad Road, is another nice little painted
site called Tollkop where an earthy-brown and dichrome series
are clearly later in date than another painting in dark claret.
In this older series were painted a number of human figures
with very fat calves, a style of drawing often found in sites by
the Great Kei, as well as near Dordrecht at Clark's Siding
and Victory Farm.

A couple of miles from Dordrecht, beyond the vlei, there is
a small rock-shelter where to-day cattle are herded. High up
on the back wall of the shelter a magnificent isolated figure of an
elephant (Fig. XXII) is painted in dark claret. It measures some
2 feet 7 inches by 1 foot 6 inches. To reach the elephant it is
necessary to scramble up to a ledge some 6 feet or so above the
level of the ground. Still more—alas! sadly destroyed—paintings
can be found close to the town in the Kloof. As usual in all these
rock-shelters an Upper Smithfield industry can be collected.
Sometimes the little scrapers are rather small, somewhat resembling those found in the Wilton industries, but similar
scrapers appear throughout in typical Smithfield sites and no
crescents or other pigmies were discovered.

Queenstown is another excellent centre from the point of
view of art, painted localities occurring both in the vicinity
along the Black Kei and near Tarkastad. The most interesting
sites we examined were close to the little village of Tylden
about 50 miles from Queenstown on the railway to East

PLATE VI

Painted site at Camp Siding, Tylden.

The main rock-shelter at Wilton.

London. Just below the village on the left bank of the Black Kei a small krantz is seen where a number of paintings occupy several niches in a low, long rock-shelter which faces south. The colours seen were dark claret and black, and there were polychromes in which white, black and orange were used.

In the first niche is a large man painted in dark claret. He is apparently running and has a sort of "Phrygian" cap on his head. To the right are a number of polychrome elands, and a man and an elephant in black. Superpositions show the black elephant over a dark claret man, a polychrome eland over dark claret punctuations and a double superposition consisting of a poorly drawn dichrome (dark claret and black) over a black man shooting with a bow which again is over a poorly drawn dark orange figure with a deeper reddish outline. In another niche to the right there is a beautifully drawn painting in black of a steatopygous man; also another of a black man with an animal.

A mile or two away from Tylden on the Queenstown Road is a farm close to Camp Siding. Below the homestead in a krantz (Plate VI), down by a small tributary stream of the Black Kei, is an extraordinarily interesting site with innumerable paintings. There are polychromes showing yellow, yellow-green, orange, white, black or dark claret, and paintings in most of these colours used separately. Superpositions show:

Polychrome	Yellow	White
Dark claret	Dark claret	Dark claret

As elsewhere this dark claret series is the earlier and several interesting observations can be made about it at this site. Human figures with fat, exaggerated calves, already observed at Tollkop and common on the Great Kei, occur prominently (Fig. XXIII); there are also some very neat outline drawings in a similar style. These singularly attractive figures are probably unfinished and no doubt it was the intention of the artist to fill in the outlines with colour later on. As a possible indication of his method of working these figures are interesting[1]. Some of them have "fringes," possibly meant to represent

[1] Compare Readman's Farm (p. 128).

hair, hanging from them. Unlike those at Modderpoort they are here painted in the same dark claret colour as the rest of the figures (Fig. XXIII). There were scenes and groups made up of these fat-calved figures, but we were only able to guess at their significance. Several queer unintelligible signs were also noted (Fig. XXIV, 2). In the later, polychrome series there was a delightful scene of a man apparently feeding an eland with aloes. In this case only two legs of the eland are shown, and the body is painted in yellowish-green (Fig. XXIII). This was the only polychrome of this kind that we saw. The green body is outlined in yellow and the hoofs and horns are indicated in black. Slightly nearer the homestead, but within the main rock-shelter, an overhanging rock can be seen with a small panel below it showing a number of human beings, rather feathery in appearance. One painting of a man facing a buffalo somewhat recalls the famous scene at Cogul in north-east Spain. This whole panel belongs to the dark claret series.

In a little krantz further down the stream is another site, where a number of similar paintings occur. The interest here is in their position rather than in the paintings themselves, for they occur high up above a narrow ledge and can only be reached after a considerable scramble, the last 4 feet being perpendicular and the ledge itself so narrow and the cliff so overhanging that it is almost impossible to stand upright. While it is conceivable that a hunter might sleep on the ledge with the assurance of safety from wild animals, one would have thought this security would have been counterbalanced by the danger of rolling over and falling off into the river bed below. But what is certain is that this site could in no sense of the word have been a home. A small figure of interest was that of a steatopygous woman in dark claret and some other figures in the same colour overlaid by paintings in earthy-yellow.

On Ella's Farm, near Queenstown, in a rock-shelter in a small krantz down by a little stream there were one or two interesting paintings, some human beings with bows being depicted (Fig. XXIV).

About 7 miles from Queenstown, beyond the dam, on the

A group of dark claret figures at Camp Siding, Tylden.

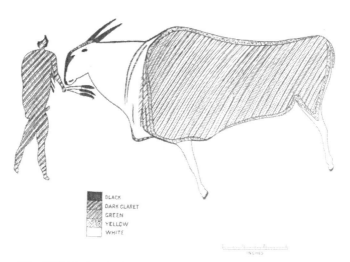

BLACK
DARK CLARET
GREEN
YELLOW
WHITE

Fig. XXIII. A polychrome painting of a man feeding an eland
at Camp Siding, Tylden.

hill behind the homestead of Rockwood Farm, there occur a number of immense boulders which frequently form rock-shelters. In many of these paintings occur. In one instance a most peculiar panel is seen, the paint looking very fresh and having all the appearance of modern distemper. The drawings consist of geometric figures, squares, circles, crosses, dots, irregular rectangles, and combinations of these. One drawing may have been intended to represent a cart laid flat with the wheels spread out on each side as if seen from above. The age of these paintings and the identity of the artists are quite unknown, but judging from the appearance of the paintings they cannot be of any great antiquity, although at the homestead no tradition survives concerning them.

Near Tarkastad we noted some delightful paintings of which the black ostrich reproduced in Fig. XXII is an example.

Space does not permit a description of every rock-shelter that we visited and only the more important ones have been mentioned. Nor has it been possible in this book of general interest to enumerate all the figures to be seen at each site. Such a catalogue would at present serve no useful purpose and would only tire the reader. Still, enough has perhaps been said in the foregoing notes about some few sites to show the sort of data on which the following observations about the paintings of this Central Art Group, as we may call it, are based.

Firstly, its distribution is intimately bound up with the geographical features of the country described in Chapter II. Examples of it are found round the mountain massif of the Drakensberg on both the eastern and western slopes. Where this massif breaks up and turns westward they are found among its hilly slopes towards the interior of the country in the Orange Free State and Cape Province. The most westward site recorded is said to be near Ladismith in the Little Karroo. They do not cross the extensions of the mountain ranges which run along more or less parallel to the south coast. In this respect their distribution coincides with that of the Smithfield culture and it is with industries of this kind that they are always found associated.

A group of purple figures at a site on Ella's Farm, near Queenstown.

INCHES

Fig. XXIV. 1. A group of dark claret figures in another rock-shelter in the same krantz on Ella's Farm. 2. A queer composite sign painted in dark claret at Camp Siding, Tylden.

The types of paintings in this art group are much more varied and give one the impression that they are much more modern than those of Southern Rhodesia. Partly perhaps for these reasons, and partly because time was lacking, we did not make such a complete study of the superpositions as we had done further north. But also because it seemed clear that superpositions were of much less importance in this region—for polychrome painting allows of so many possibilities that we could not make out a definite sequence of styles in it, except as regards its evolution and degeneration which we have already discussed. It was significant, however, that, whenever paintings comparable in colour and style to the dark claret or middle series of Rhodesia occurred in superposition with any other styles or colours in this art group, they were always the undermost and therefore the oldest.

I think further investigation will show that various local geographical art centres within this Central Group evolved independently slightly different styles from those developed in other centres. Such centres may prove to be for instance the Drakensberg district; the Kei River district so well studied by Brother Otto (30); or again the modern group round Molteno. Even in the present state of our knowledge a student of the art, if shown a good reproduction of some paintings should, within reasonable limits, be able to say to which district they should be referred.

Besides the wonderful polychrome developments an important feature, distinguishing the paintings of this group from those of Southern Rhodesia, is the frequent occurrence of elaborate scenes. Even painted stories (48, plate 8, no. 23)—which according to Miss Bleek are illustrative of Bushman folk legends—occur, and as at Tylden complicated, if inexplicable, scenes are often to be observed, while cattle-stealing pictures are common. In Rhodesia, where, except for the somewhat anomalous Impey group, we saw no true scenes, it was at best only simple groups that were depicted, and these but rarely.

ROCK ENGRAVINGS (52)

Here, on account of its distribution, we must consider briefly another manifestation of the prehistoric art of South Africa, namely the rock engravings. Unfortunately these are restricted to certain areas, being generally confined to the central parts of the country north and west of the mountain chains. This does not mean to say that rock engravings are unknown elsewhere; indeed they have been found, for example, in the Gaub district of what was formerly German South-West Africa and elsewhere[1]; but they are by far the most frequently met with and far more uniform in appearance in the central districts of the Orange Free State and the adjoining northern parts of the Cape Province which lie immediately to the west. This distribution coincides more or less with an area rich in dolerite, the rock upon which the engravings are usually made. It does sometimes happen that other varieties of rock are engraved, as for example certain fine-grained granites in the Kenhardt district. But dolerite is a material very suitable for the purpose, being at the same time hard and fine-grained, and it is in regions where it occurs that thousands of engravings have been found and thousands more remain to be discovered.

Dolerite patinates readily, the colour of the patina being almost brick red; it is this which produces the wonderful sunset effects in the Karroo when the mountain chains of dolerite become a flood of gold or a flame of fire. Further patination produces a deep mahogany colour which is sometimes even lustrous.

Visitors to Capetown, Kimberley, Pretoria, etc., will often notice in the museums examples of rock engravings that have been flaked off from dolerite boulders and deposited there. As might be expected, however, only the most striking examples have, as a rule, been chosen and these are by no

[1] Some interesting figures, probably intended to represent spoors of animals, occur in this district. Similar engravings have been discovered lately, carved on some flat rocks in Northern Rhodesia, close to the Congo border, and others have been found engraved on the walls of a small cave in Southern Rhodesia in the neighbourhood of Wankie (33).

means always the most interesting or the earliest. On examination at any one locality, various kinds of techniques and styles
can be determined much in the same way as in the case of the
paintings.

Though a large number of engravings were seen in the
course of our tour it was two widely separated sites both
covered with such engravings that were most thoroughly
studied. The first of these was in the Karroo near Vosberg
(p. 30), and the other was Afvallingskop (p. 40), close by
the township of Koffiefontein in the Orange Free State.
Animals of various kinds are depicted and not infrequently
human beings can be noted. Besides these there are a number
of signs of various kinds which are not always easy to inter-
pret. Some of these may be fanciful representations of flowers
and of snakes. Others are certainly more geometric and pattern-
like in appearance.

On the summit of the decorated kopje near Vosberg a large
boulder, much undercut, had doubtless been used as a shelter,
and there we found a Smithfield industry. Although the contemporaneity of this with the engravings (Fig. XXV) cannot be
proved it would seem probable that at least some of the series
which we are going to describe are the work of Smithfield
man. Four distinct techniques almost certainly of very different
ages can be determined as follows[1]:

Engravings of the earliest series show a fine incised outline
and the bodies of the animals are filled in with fine lines more
or less parallel to this outline (Fig. XXV, 1). In some cases
the surface of the engravings has almost the appearance of

[1] Since I left Africa Mr Goodwin has acceded to my earnest request
and is seriously taking up the study of this interesting site with a view to
a detailed publication later on. Another group of engravings was discovered by him on a kopje near by and his further studies seem not only
to confirm the evidence that we discovered but also to amplify it. Whether
this amplification is only of local importance or whether it can be applied
to a wide area cannot yet be stated with certainty. A lot of detailed work
on many other sites is required before this can be determined. Only broad
outlines are given in this volume and these will probably be found to be
applicable to all the rock engravings of the central region.

Fig. XXV. Rock engravings at Vosberg. 1. An example of Series I.
2. Examples of the "pocked outline" style, Series II.

having been rubbed over later, but this may be partly due to subsequent weathering. The important fact to notice is that the patina of the engraved lines is exactly as dark as that of the rock on which the figure is engraved. This indeed often makes it very difficult to see the figures, and it is not to be wondered at that examples of the incised style are not seen in museum collections. At Vosberg we noted elephant and eland figured in this series.

Another series comprised figures of animals made by a pocking technique without any definite outline; sometimes there is merely an outline formed by a more or less wide band of coarse pockings (Fig. XXV. 2); sometimes the whole of the body of the animal, sometimes the head and neck only, are covered with pock marks. This pocking technique clearly shows that a punch was used, and in view of the hard nature of the dolerite one would imagine that punches must have been made by shaping some still harder pebble to produce a sort of cigar-shaped point. But no such tools, or indeed any tool suitable for making these engravings, has yet been found. The patina of this second series is not quite so deep as it is in the case of Series I; on this ground alone we came to the conclusion that the pocking technique here was invariably rather more modern than the incised technique of Series I. A variation of Series II can be recognised where the pock marks, instead of being little more or less circular hollows, consist of dashes. It is quite easy to see how this variation probably arose. If the punching was effected by means of direct blows at right angles to the rock, the normal kind of pocking would result. If, however, the punch were held obliquely to the rock surface there would result a long dash in place of the circular pock mark. Generally, the body of the animal is covered all over with such dashes, but less densely than in the case of the normal pocking. The patina is similar. In Series II we noted figures of eland, springbok and rhinoceros.

Series III is the most important and the most frequently seen of all, and, judging from the fact that the patina is sometimes fairly deep and sometimes very slight, it must have lasted through

PLATE VII

Engraving of a giraffe in the "dashes" style at Pniel.

Painted hands, near Riversdale, typical of the Southern (Wilton) Art Group.
N.B. The spottiness over the hands is due to a defect in the negative.

a long period of time. Especially when only slightly patinated, the drawings are lighter in colour than the patinated surface of the rock itself, and are therefore very visible. Engravings of this series show a clear outline, the body of the animal being, as it were, deeply rubbed all over. That this "rubbing" was done with a fine punch making a minute pocking all over the surface, seems to me to be proved by the fact that definite pock marks can occasionally be made out. Buck, ostrich and eland are figured, and also some metal spears which occur in superposition over the body of an elephant belonging to Series I. This fact is important from two points of view. Firstly, because here stratigraphy confirms the deductions obtained from a study of the preservation, i.e. degree of patination; such a confirmation is necessary, for of course weathering is always a capricious factor, although the engravings being all in the open and close together, and the rocks being all of the same material, it generally forms a fairly safe guide. Secondly, because the occurrence of what must have been meant for metal spears indicates that a part, at least, of this third series only dates back as far as the introduction of metal into South Africa, which was due, in the first instance, to the Hottentots (41).

Lastly, at Vosberg we noted a series showing no patina and made in various ways, generally with a metal knife; this was clearly the work of modern herdsmen, doubtless in imitation of the older engravings around. The bodies of the animals are sometimes filled in with cross-hatching, an uncommon feature in the earlier series.

Another interesting site we visited was at Pniel on the Vaal river some little distance from Kimberley. No examples of the early series were observed here, but among many engravings in the pocked style of Series II a very fine figure of a giraffe (Plate VII), with body pocked all over, was especially noted. On the way to Pniel, at the "Halfway House" (p. 33), the rocks on the kopje itself are covered with engravings, but here again I noted no example of Series I, and I am not sure whether even Series II was represented; probably most of the art there should be assigned to Series III.

Afvallingskop (Figs. XXVI, XXVII and XXVIII) is far higher and steeper than the kopje at Vosberg; it is beautifully situated near the Riet river and is very conspicuous.

Here, as at Vosberg, the earliest series consists of outlined drawings, the lines being incised and the body of the animal partially filled in with lines more or less parallel to the outline. The patina is that of the rock itself, and in every respect the technique and style are exactly similar to those of Series I at Vosberg. Among the species of animals figured are buffaloes and baboons. A variant of this series, however, seems to occur where the outlined drawing was made first, and the body then lightly pocked all over, the pocking not always coinciding with the outline, just as is the case with a cheap coloured print when the register is not perfect. The patina, however, is that of the rock and it would not be possible to separate this variation from Series I. In technique, it forms a sort of link between Series I and Series II. In Series II we have the "pocked outline" and the "dashes" variant just as at Vosberg, and also, as at Vosberg, the patina is deep, though not quite so deep as that of the rock. Fortunately at Afvallingskop an actual superposition was discovered between this series and Series I, for part of an outlined drawing is covered by an animal in the "dashes" style (Fig. XXVII).

In Series III (Fig. XXVI, 2) the animals are made by a fine pocking, so fine indeed that it is almost as though the surface of the figure had been rubbed over with sand-paper. As a rule no incised outline occurs, but the punch marks are so neat that the first impression given is as of a sharp silhouette clearly defined. In one example, however, the belly of an animal was actually formed by an incised line, which shows that such an outline was sometimes first drawn. Generally the whole of the figure of the animal is treated, but some examples occur where part of the body is left unworked (Fig. XXVIII). As in the case of Series III at Vosberg the patina varies, but is never very deep, and again, as at the former site, this series is the commonest and probably persisted through a long period.

Lastly, quite a number of modern herdsman drawings were

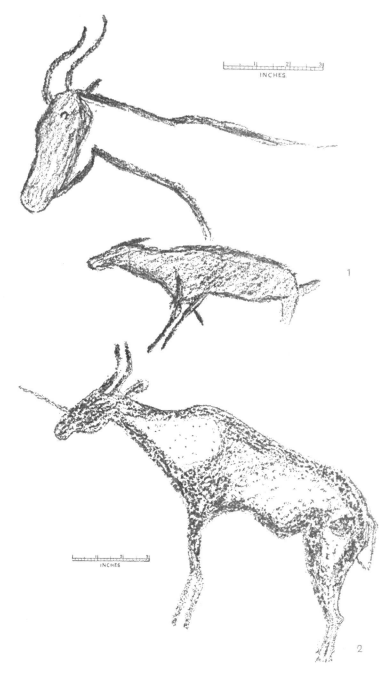

INCHES

INCHES

Fig. XXVI. Engravings at Afvallingskop. 1. An example of Series I.
2. An example of Series III.

noted and in this series occurs a figure which is undoubtedly connected with such a game as "Nine Men's Morris." As at Vosberg, the figures belonging to this series are mostly made with a metal knife. A few indeterminate stone implements were found on the kopje and at its base, but nothing so typical as the industry discovered at Vosberg.

PAINTINGS OF THE SOUTHERN GROUP

Leaving the country of the Central Art Group we crossed the mountains and came down into the coastal belt alluded to in Chapter III. Here the rock-shelter art proved to be of such a completely different nature from anything we had before seen that I have ventured to class it as a third group, calling it the Southern or Wilton Art Group, for it is with tools of the Wilton culture that we invariably find it associated. The paintings of this group are totally dissimilar from and far inferior in style and technique to the paintings of the central group. They are, however, amazingly similar to one another even in widely separated areas, and when examining paintings at sites near Grahamstown it is astonishing to find that they are identical counterparts of paintings as far away as Riversdale, several hundred miles further westwards.

The Southern Art Group does not know polychromes. Together with the Smithfield industries we have left the gay herds of elands of the Central Art Group behind the mountains. The figures are for the most part executed in a uniform bright red, almost vermilion colour, and the rock background itself is frequently also reddened and smudgy as well. The animals are very poorly drawn and the figures of human beings are often large and angular. The human hand is represented again and again, a fact which is never the case in the Central Art Group and, so far as I know, has never been noted in Southern Rhodesia. Both left and right hands are depicted; they show no signs of mutilation and are strikingly small—far smaller than those of average-sized white women. However, this is not surprising. The Bushfolk were a tiny race.

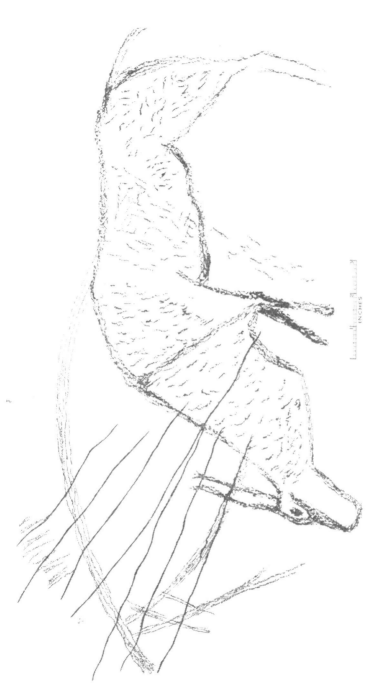

Fig. XXVII. Engravings at Afvallingskop showing superpositions of styles. The animal in the "dashes" style is superposed on a band of engraved lines of the earliest style, but is itself crossed by modern unpatinated lines.

A number of interesting sites were visited some 6 miles from Grahamstown. They are on Glencraig Farm, in a krantz above the Botha river to the left of the road to King Williamstown, just where it crosses the river. No clear superpositions were observed and the paintings are probably all of about the same age. Not all the human figures, however, appear to be Bushman; there is one with a long lance, tipped with a little spear-head, which probably represents a Bantu. The Bushmen also depicted themselves, however, and an example was seen in the "on all fours" position. A great many typical Wilton tools were collected from these sites.

At Wilton (Plate VI) itself similar paintings, including several representations of the human hand (Fig. XXIX, 3), occur with the smudgy reddened background. Some of them are certainly very modern, sheep being depicted, but these latter, which are painted in a sort of thick white colour, are rather more recent than the bright red figures on which they are in one or two instances superposed. Below the actual Wilton rock-shelter and further down the valley is another containing, among other drawings, a rather interesting net-like figure.

Further westwards an interesting site where paintings of the Wilton Art Group occur is situated about 7 miles from Riversdale. The rock-shelter is high up in a krantz on the right bank of a small stream some distance to the right of the Riversdale-Ladismith Road. A side road which turns off the main road just after a river has been crossed must be followed; it leads to a farm whence a mile of rough walking and scrambling brings one to the shelter. It is much concealed by bushes, measures about 24 yards by 12 yards (maximum measurements), and faces south-east. The paintings are in bright red on a similar background, the whole of the back wall of the rock-shelter being so reddened. Especially to be noticed is the enormous number of small hands (Plate VII and Fig. XXIX) here represented, which has led to the shelter being named the Cave of the Hands. Some half-dozen insignificant figures of animals and humans and a few rather darker coloured dots, perhaps of a slightly later age, were also noted. A vast number of typical Wilton tools have been

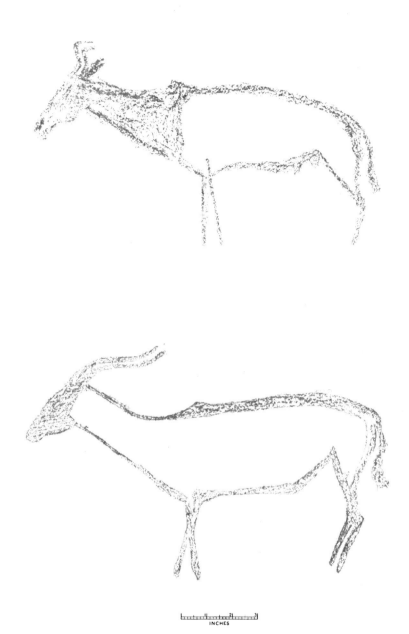

INCHES

Fig. XXVIII. Two engravings at Afvallingskop, perhaps belonging to Series II, or possibly variants of Series III.

excavated by Mr Heese, our host, from the floor of the rock-shelter.

Still further westwards paintings have been recorded in the Clan William district which, judging from copies sketched in an old notebook[1], would seem to belong, for the most part, to the Wilton Art Group.

Few helpful superpositions occurred in this group, for the artists hardly seem to have realised the possibilities of any other colour but red, and we did not observe any paintings which could be considered as forming a link with the Central Art Group. The reddened background, against which the outlines of the figures painted in the same colour were hard to distinguish, was peculiar and very characteristic. Notable, too, were the very powdery deposits which formed the floor of all the Wilton painted rock-shelters that we visited and in which the Wilton industries were found.

As regards the motives which prompted the execution of the paintings or engravings, little can be said. My own impression is that they were mixed and not necessarily similar at all periods. Rival schools of thought hold two different views on this subject: the one considering that all the art was made and used for magic or ceremonial purposes; the other that it was merely the outward expression of an artistic people filling in the chance half-hours of a somewhat monotonous existence, or in some cases that the paintings were actual decorations, in the way of "wall-papers," for the rock-shelter homes.

It is interesting to note that generally I found the exponents of the latter school were people who had mainly had dealings with the rock-shelter art down in the Union, while in Rhodesia several investigators were inclined to consider that the paintings had a rather deeper significance. In all probability the whole truth lies neither with the one nor with the other. The later paintings found down in the Union may, in many cases, have been merely the products of idle hours. They frequently occur in places which could have been made into comfortable homes,

[1] Now in the possession of Mrs Lister at Capetown.

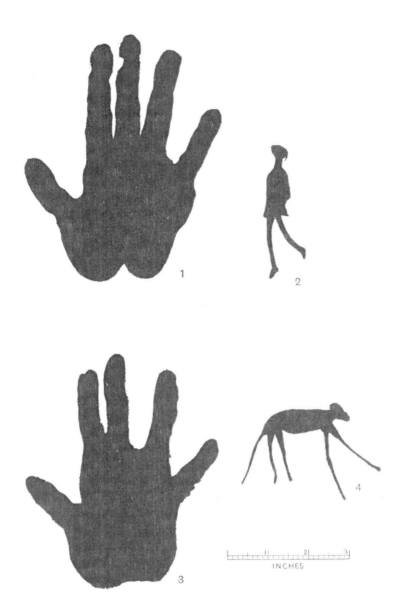

Fig. XXIX. 1 and 2. A hand and figure in the "Cave of the Hands" near Riversdale. 3. A hand at Wilton. 4. A baboon in a rock-shelter near the road and beyond the hotel at Howieson's Poort. All are painted in bright red and are examples of the Southern (Wilton) art group.

and in fact industries are often found below the floors of the rock-shelters themselves. That this is not, however, always the case reference to the second painted site near Camp Siding, Tylden, will show, and painted localities where people could never have lived are definitely known. This is, however, more often the case in Southern Rhodesia, as for example at the Beatrice Road and the M.T.C. sites near Salisbury (pp. 117, 123).

Further, the whole situation at Domboshawa, and its connection with rain production already described, must be taken into account. Even a site like Makumbi would have been very inconvenient as a permanent home owing to its distance from water. I am inclined myself to accept the view that during its earlier phases the art was definitely connected with spots where ritual acts took place, although in some cases we find examples dating from the earliest times in sites which were undoubtedly homes. Brother Otto of Mariannhill believes that several queer-shaped figures were meant to represent traps (9) (30), and as these are found associated with animals and human beings it is quite possible that some sort of magic is involved in connection with hunting. Further, Brother Otto has copied several pictures which, he considers, depict foreigners recognisable from their clothing as Malays, Chinamen, etc., gripping Bushmen by the arms as though in the act of enslaving them. Here again it is a question of a very vital crisis for the Bushman, just such a situation as might call forth a religio-magic representation (9) (30). Later on, especially southwards in the Union, it is quite likely that the older significance was somewhat lost but that painting continued because the folk themselves were artistic and expressed themselves in this way. But in this connection—when we find a scene representing a European farmer ill-treating a Bushman while in the corner two little Bushmen are shooting at him with bows and arrows—are we merely to see a reproduction of an actual occurrence or may we not read into it something in the nature of a magic or a painted prayer (24) that the arrows shot by the little men in the corner may hit their mark?

Turning to the engravings, the difficulty of interpretation if anything increases. It would hardly seem likely that these often isolated, windswept kopje tops can have been homes, and one wonders again whether they were not meeting-places where some definite rites took place, the spots being decorated or sanctified for much the same reason as many of our churches and public buildings are decorated to-day. At " Halfway House " it is true the engravings are found at a site where a Bushman village is said to have been, although, of course, there is no absolute proof that any connection existed between it and the engravings.

CHAPTER X

ZIMBABWE

NO account of South Africa's past would be complete without some mention of the extraordinarily interesting ruins which have been discovered in Southern Rhodesia. In many places, especially at Zimbabwe, which lies some 17 miles or so from Fort Victoria, there are to be seen the ruins of imposing buildings showing considerable skill in construction. They form to-day a more or less imperfect chain stretching across Southern Rhodesia, and many of the links in the chain, not at present known, will be discovered when the country becomes more thickly populated and better explored.

Controversy has long raged as to their age and the culture to which they should be assigned. One school of thought considers that they date back to a very remote period indeed and that they were due to early Phoenician traders who had penetrated down the east coast of Africa and far into the interior of what is now Rhodesia in quest of the gold which is found in the country. Mr Hall strongly upholds this view in his books (22 23). Other people, however, consider that they are much more recent; in fact that they were only destroyed a comparatively short time before the Portuguese first set foot on the shore at Capetown, if not later still. I hesitate to do more than sketch briefly my own impressions of Zimbabwe, more especially as I hold strongly to this latter view and therefore consider that the whole question is really outside the scope of this book and certainly of my own competence.

One point, however, I should like to stress, namely that the intrinsic interest of Zimbabwe and other similar ruins is in no way lessened by assigning to them a rather more recent date. They are, and always will remain, peculiar monuments of extraordinary importance whoever made them and whenever they were made.

At Zimbabwe there are three distinct areas where constructions occur:

(1) The acropolis.

(2) The so-called temple.

(3) The lesser ruins in the valley.

The acropolis (Plate VIII) is built on a granite kopje, many natural huge rounded boulders being incorporated in the constructions. The kopje is very precipitous, especially on the side facing the "temple," where it falls down sheer for a considerable distance. Access in ancient days was gained by a narrow stairway which often winds between immense granite boulders and must have been easy to defend against attack. A sort of flat platform on the edge of the kopje was partly enclosed by high walls, whence the interior was reached by means of narrow passages through the wall. Behind, other parts of the kopje show similar, but smaller, constructions, with small chambers and passages abounding. The walls themselves are made from granite blocks which are as a matter of fact easily obtained, for the great natural granite domes of the district scale off, the scalings being only a few inches thick, so that all the builders had to do was to break such scalings up into roughly rectangular bricks. It is significant that just around Zimbabwe most of the natural scalings seem to have disappeared, doubtless having been removed for the construction of the building.

On the top of the acropolis wall, which is some 4 feet or more thick, there are three or four peculiar conical turrets which have given rise to much controversy. At a distance the walls seem to have been built in regular courses of granite bricks, but a nearer view shows that in reality the construction is distinctly irregular. Straight lines are conspicuous by their absence. For example, the little conical turrets are not pyramidal, as might have been expected, but are constructed throughout on a "curved batter," so characteristic of modern Bantu constructions. No form of mortar occurs.

As I was leaving Salisbury, Mr Maufe, of the Geological Survey in Southern Rhodesia, had advised me to pay particular attention to the deposits occurring inside the acropolis wall. These consist of a soft, red earthy material full of fragments of pottery exactly similar in every respect to that made by the Bantu to-day. Further, the origin of this deposit was perfectly clear, for a large number of round beaten floors occurred therein, similar to those that are yearly hammered down by the Bantus in their circular kraals. In other words the whole deposit consists of a sequence of Kaffir hearths. The upper layers of this deposit have also yielded many gold objects, etc., as the investigations of previous diggers have shown.

As has been said, the ground falls sheer on the temple side and here the wall is built on the cliff edge, as it were continuing the precipice. On the outer side it is evenly and well constructed, much care having been taken in the building; on the inner side the construction is very much rougher. We noted the important fact that the bottom two or three feet of the Kaffir hearths mentioned above disappeared underneath the inner margin of the wall. Further in these hearths, and vertically below the wall, I myself excavated a fragment of what seemed to me to be, and was passed by Mr Goodwin as being, a sherd of ordinary Bantu pottery. What seems to have happened is this: the deposits made by the Kaffirs accumulated on this flat shelf of the kopje, doubtless rather thicker in the middle and thinning down to nothing at the edge of the precipice. A little later the wall was constructed, being built on the rock itself at the edge of the cliff, but over the earlier Kaffir hearth deposits on its inner margin. Later the interior of the enclosure was filled in by the further accumulation of Kaffir hearths.

There is evidence to show that the Bantu only reached Bechuanaland in the course of the 14th century of our era; and, in all probability, they were not in Southern Rhodesia much before 900 A.D. Stratigraphical evidence therefore argues for a date some time after 900 A.D. for the building of the wall. But Zimbabwe had been destroyed some time before the Europeans first penetrated the country and written accounts were made. In this region, however, through which fresh waves of move-

PLATE VIII

ZIMBABWE.
View of the acropolis from the "temple."

ZIMBABWE.
View inside the "temple" showing the big conical tower.

ment must have been continually coming from the north and penetrating southwards, legends of these ruined monuments would not necessarily have long survived. Various peoples kept a certain record of their own history, but not necessarily an account of the ruins in a country into which they had penetrated, or even of buildings that they had helped to destroy. It might seem reasonable then to suggest some date lying between 1000 A.D. and 1200 A.D. for their construction and use.

But several other problems remain to be elucidated about these ruins. Even if such a date is correct, who were the builders, why were they built, and if the mining of gold and precious metals was the motive whither was the spoil exported? The fact that everything is built on a curved batter argues strongly that the actual builders were Kaffirs. On the other hand, judging from the present peoples, it is almost inconceivable that these immense constructions could have been planned and designed by them. It would appear more likely that a foreign influence invaded the country and caused local labour to set up these buildings for purposes of defence and otherwise. If the foreigners only penetrated occasionally to fetch from the fortified places the "loot" collected for them by the natives and did not actually live in the land with their wives and children, we should not expect to find in the present local inhabitants many traces, physical or otherwise, left by these invaders of a former age. That gold was the magnet which attracted the outsider is undoubted; it can be got by alluvial digging and also by mining, and immense quantities must have been accumulated in a comparatively short time. Major Tudor Trevor, who has made a study of the prehistoric mines, assures me that while seventy million pounds sterling is of course an exaggeration, ten or fifteen million pounds is by no means out of the picture as a figure for such an accumulation. The chain of forts that are found in Southern Rhodesia, of which Zimbabwe is the greatest, must have been essential to ensure the safe storing, smelting and perhaps exporting of the precious metal.

It would seem unlikely that Europeans took any hand in this matter. If they had been the dominating and invading people, then the gold would have been exported to Europe. This can hardly have been the case as at no time before the 19th century could such a mass of bullion have been introduced into Europe, in what would seem to have been a comparatively short time, without showing evident traces of its presence in a rapid change in the value of the currency and in a great increase in the number of gold ornaments, etc. In the 9th century Scandinavians spread over northern Russia and even took tribute from Byzantium, but in this case a study of the graves shows that there was a remarkable increase in the number of gold ornaments in the funeral furniture of the time. It may be that the Southern Rhodesian gold was traded with India and that part of the bullion now hoarded by some of the great Rajahs of that land may have originally come to their ancestors from Africa. In that case the traders, if they were not Indians, might have been Arabs who, since the growth of Islam, had penetrated down the east coast of Africa and there formed isolated and independent kingdoms. Of these very little authentic history survives and it would seem quite possible that one of their sources of wealth and the object of their activities was trading with the natives of the interior, and naturally if gold was to be had, it would be a much sought-after commodity. However, the absence at Zimbabwe of any traces of Arabic inscriptions rather militates against the theory of an Arab penetration.

Finally, the uprising of some tribe under a now forgotten leader must have driven out the merchant invaders, whoever they were and, for reasons unknown, the traffic was never again restarted.

The "temple" is built down in the valley; it is oval in shape and consists of an immense high wall inclosing numerous inner walls. Entrance is gained by narrow gateways in the wall, the rounded ends of which form high protecting towers, while in the interior the most striking feature is an isolated conical tower (Plate VIII). There are other smaller conical towers, but the big one is by far the most imposing. It can be reached by a narrow gloomy passage formed by a second wall within and parallel to the outer wall. An interesting chevron-pattern decoration appears at the top of the outer wall, which certainly seems to indicate foreign influence. The exact purpose which this so-called "temple" served is not clearly known.

At the bottom of the valley there are a number of ruined constructions, seemingly houses and the like, also what may have been miniature oval "temples" of less elaborate internal construction.

It must not be supposed, however, that the problem of Zimbabwe is yet in any way solved. What is needed is a well-equipped expedition of competent diggers to excavate on a large scale over a number of seasons. Hitherto the materials obtained have been derived from sporadic diggings, which have yielded many important finds comprising gold rings, pottery, and especially some queer soapstone rods with figures of birds carved on the end, which cannot properly be connected with any known culture. Nevertheless, what is needed is a systematic investigation and it would be interesting to see the results of excavation in the valley ruins which may have been actually "home" sites, and where finds might well indicate the identity of their owners. Again, much excavation work requires to be done in the "temple" itself and even on the acropolis the ground has only been scratched and everything remains to be done. Now that Zimbabwe is being suitably cared for and has become a resort for visitors, it would be all the more interesting to see excavation started on a large scale and the results placed in a local museum constructed on the spot. At present collections from Zimbabwe are scattered, being housed partly at Capetown, partly at Salisbury, and partly at Bulawayo.

Ruins like Zimbabwe and Khami, near Bulawayo, are by no means the only constructions of their kind which occur in Southern Rhodesia and which have been left for us as the result of some dominating influence in the country, in time past. There are also terraced constructions on the hillsides and other manifestations of the activities of organised man. These, too, need investigating, and it would be well if the inhabitants of Southern Rhodesia—that most favoured of lands—would look to the investigation of their past history before hordes of newcomers necessarily destroy much of the present evidence which lies at their doors waiting to be collected and studied.

Some of the conclusions at which we personally arrived on the spot seemed to confirm those of Mr J. F. Schofield, which were read to the South African Association for the Advancement of Science at its meeting in 1926 (42). At the time of my visit to Zimbabwe I am ashamed to say I had not read the paper in question; it is therefore all the more interesting that we should have independently felt convinced of the comparative modernity of the ruins, although his work was naturally far more detailed and prolonged than anything we could attempt. Mr Schofield is of the opinion that peoples of two cultures lived in the Zimbabwe district, but that it is to the second and later of these, the Baroswe (Barotse) that the building of most of the "temple" must be attributed. He goes so far as to consider that the building is post-mediaeval, having been begun after the Portuguese conquest. Interesting items with which he supports these conclusions are that none of the trees now growing within the "temple" are more than a hundred years old, and that the natives round about have a tradition that the buildings were erected by their ancestors who mined gold and sent it to "Mambo who lived in the Victoria district." Quite such a late date for the construction is perhaps difficult to credit as the ruins are mentioned as such by the Portuguese during their early days in South Africa. Mr Schofield came to very similar conclusions in respect to the deposits within the acropolis walls. Taken as a whole, however, it seems unlikely that the theory of a very great antiquity for the ruins can be any longer sustained.

CHAPTER XI

SUMMARY OF CONCLUSIONS

MANY of the conclusions arrived at as a result of our studies in the course of our tour have already been given in their due places with the evidence on which they are based. It is convenient, however, to collect them together here and amplify them to a certain extent; also to see where and how far the prehistory of South Africa can be linked up with that of other countries of which we have any knowledge.

It would appear that the culture of the earliest South Africans was Lower Palaeolithic. They were users of *coups de poing* and developed the Victoria West, Stellenbosch, and Fauresmith industries which we have described, the last of these being, in all probability, a late development, perhaps influenced by a Middle Palaeolithic culture. Nothing can be said as to whether this Lower Palaeolithic culture of South Africa is contemporary with or later than the Lower Palaeolithic in the North. In spite of the finding of *coups de poing* in association with mammoth teeth (10), my impression is that it is of more recent date, both in view of the enormous number of tools which survive, many of them comparatively fresh in appearance, and in view of the number of variants of the original form of *coup de poing* which can be found. It is true that, though absent in Europe, examples of most of these variants such as the Stellenbosch cleaver and the Vaal river tools described in Chapter IV can be noted in the Lower Palaeolithic industries of North Africa; but their wealth and perfection in South Africa seem to me to in-indicate either that the culture survived there undisturbed by outside influences for a very long period of time, or that after a very slow progression southwards it had arrived in the country with these variants already fully developed. Their characteristic features as well as the reasons for their manufacture were clearly determined by the nature of the material from which they were made. The southward trek probably led from the Sahara—then fertile country—which was perhaps an early home of the Lower Palaeolithic folk.

That the Mousterian or Middle Palaeolithic culture occurred widely in North Africa and probably survived there till a far later date than it did in Europe, has been shown by Professor Seligman (43). It occurs also in Somaliland. Although in South Africa I saw no sites where the industries were purely Middle Palaeolithic, it seems certain, on typological grounds, that this culture played its part in influencing the older Lower Palaeolithic culture in that country. It is possible that it was introduced by some late wave of Lower Palaeolithic peoples who had come in contact with the Mousterians in North Africa. It is fairly certain, at any rate, that it played a part in the development of the late Lower Palaeolithic Fauresmith industries. As has been seen, these industries include a number of highly patinated pointed flakes showing faceted striking platforms, which closely resemble Mousterian points in the process of manufacture; indeed, it may never have been found necessary to trim the edges at all since the tool was not made of brittle flint, but of the tougher indurated shale. Besides the Fauresmith industries there is even clearer evidence for the existence of a Middle Palaeolithic culture in South Africa at such sites as that near the Glengrey Falls where an almost pure Middle Palaeolithic industry occurs. The admixture, however, this time is seemingly with Neoanthropic elements instead of with Lower Palaeolithic elements. Typologically speaking the industry at Glengrey is decisive. Whether any Middle Palaeolithic influence can be traced in the evolution of the Smithfield culture may be doubted, although certain tools somewhat resembling Mousterian types do occur in Lower Smithfield industries.

That there was a Neoanthropic invasion of South Africa in pre-Wilton times is clear from the discoveries made at Bambata (Southern Rhodesia) and at Howieson's Poort. I was astonished on seeing the finds brought back by Mr Leakey from Elementeita in Kenya to note their exact similarity in every respect to those of the industry at Howieson's Poort near Grahamstown. Doubtless the cradle of the Neoanthropic race was somewhere in North Africa in those districts of the Sahara which, though now desert, were at the end of Quaternary times, fertile lands lying in a rainbelt which, owing to the presence of a glacial epoch in the north, was situated much further south than it now is. Mr Leakey is strongly of the opinion that the Nile formed a real barrier to any extensive eastward movement, and he suggests that the line of southward migration passed just to the west of the Victoria Nyanza along the high ground between it and the impenetrable forests of the Congo basin. Apparently the country would have been satisfactory for such a trek, and although it has not yet been properly explored from an archaeological point of view, a very large number of pre-historic sites including a great many painted rock-shelters are known which will doubtless yield a rich harvest to the investigator. It will be very important to see whether the style of these paintings corresponds to that of the earlier series in Southern Rhodesia. Should this be the case definite links will have been forged between Southern Rhodesia and Uganda and the Southern Sahara. In this connection it may be noted that a cave with paintings in a somewhat similar style has lately been discovered in this latter area, situated near the Tropic of Cancer and 8° West Longitude (11)[1]. This discovery in turn connects the art of our area with that of East Spain, where the paintings at Cogul (2), Alpéra (4), Barranco de Valltorta (39), Albarracin (3), etc. (Fig. xxx) very closely resemble the "Bushman" art, or, to be more accurate, the earlier series of paintings found in Southern Rhodesia. The age of the art of the eastern Spanish group is presumed to be Late Quaternary (contemporary with, though quite distinct from, the later phases of the well-known Cave Art of North Spain and southern France) as drawings of animals long since extinct in the district in question have been recognised. This is not at all incompatible with the notion that North Africa was the cradle of the Neoanthropic race and that the eastern Spanish art was attributable to a small early north-ward migration, which clung to the eastern side of Spain and failed to penetrate the Pyrenees. When the term Neoanthropic

[1] Rock-shelter art of various kinds is common in northern Africa (15).

race is used it must be remembered that in all probability developments were taking place from the earliest times and doubtless there very soon existed a number of different tribes, not all of them of quite the same culture or with quite the same physical characteristics. The Capsians (38) of the north coasts of Africa were part and parcel of these peoples, and the Howieson's Poort folk represent the final stage of a southward trek which was induced no doubt by the increasing dryness of the climate which forced the inhabitants to quit the cradle of their race.

As regards the Still Bay culture, I believe that it is a hybrid resulting from a contact of this Neoanthropic invasion with the earlier peoples in South Africa, and I suggest that the Middle Palaeolithic influence already mentioned played a part in the evolution of the special Still Bay type of lancehead (p. 86). As has been described, Colonel Hardy's researches have demonstrated this development in all its stages from what in Europe would be described as a pure Mousterian point to what at first sight would be taken to be a Solutrean laurel leaf. This is a most interesting and significant piece of work, and it may be that in general the formation of a laurel leaf type of tool is due to contact between Neoanthropic and Middle Palaeolithic cultures. Mr Leakey has found a similar state of affairs in Kenya and the same is the case in North Africa and perhaps too in Hungary, the cradle of the true Solutrean culture. That a contact between the two cultures so often seems to develop this useful type of tool cannot be too strongly urged. It means that the laurel leaf is not indicative of the Solutrean culture properly so-called, except when it is found associated with Quaternary fauna in Europe north of the Alps. As further proof that the Still Bay culture is essentially South African, and an autochthonous growth, the fact can be noted that true and typical Still Bay sites are all found in the extreme south of the continent[1].

---

[1] It will be most interesting to learn whether or not the skull discovered by Mr Peers in the cave near Fish Hoek, associated with Still Bay implements, is found to be similar to the human remains discovered at Elementeita in Kenya.

Fig. XXX. Examples of the rock-shelter art of East Spain. The figures of animals are from El Arabi, Yecla : the figures of humans are from the Barranco de Valltorta, Castellón and Alpéra.

Turning next to the Wilton culture of South Africa we find that it corresponds exactly with an industry found at Nakuru in Kenya which is later than and separated from the Elementeita finds by a whole cycle of climatic changes. In between, in Uganda, has been found the Magosi industry, discovered by Mr Wayland (51), which is also of exactly the same type. The only difficulty is, that in all probability the Wilton culture was introduced into South Africa by the Bushman folk, and in Kenya the associated human remains at Nakuru are by no means of a Bushman type. Undoubtedly there remains here a problem requiring further investigation, more especially as not far away there also existed a pigmy race, apparently contemporary with the Nakuru folk and using a similar industry. It would be very interesting to find skeletons associated with the Magosi industries in Uganda and further south. At any rate, as we have seen, the Wilton culture arrived in a pure state in Southern Rhodesia and thence penetrated over much of the Union, being especially prevalent in the extreme south where it is frequently associated with paintings of the Southern or Wilton Art group.

The Smithfield culture, which is frequently found with paintings of the Central Art Group and with rock engravings, has a distribution restricted to the Union. This is distinctly peculiar, as from a typological point of view the industries seem to show influences from a number of different cultures. Some of the side-scrapers one would almost call Mousterian, some of the concavo-convex side-scrapers are absolutely Badarian, i.e., pre-dynastic Egyptian, as also are some of the small needle-like tools. Yet industries belonging to this culture are never found north of Mafeking and are undoubtedly very modern. My impression is that the Smithfield, like the Still Bay culture, is an autochthonous growth, and may have been due to contact between the Wilton invaders and the older inhabitants of the country, possibly the folk of the Fauresmith culture. This perhaps gave rise to the Lower Smithfield culture which rapidly developed into an Upper Smithfield culture which existed until a century or so ago. Does the similarity of the Badarian concavo-convex type of tool to the implements found in the

Smithfield culture involve any cultural connection between the two? Was the knowledge of this method of forming a blade brought south by the Wilton folk, although not used by them? Their industry is mainly a pigmy one and they did not employ large pieces of indurated shale for tool making. It is impossible to say, and room must always be allowed for a similarity of types without there being any cultural connection between them[1].

Finally, for reasons already stated, I am not prepared to accept the view that all the Kitchen Midden industries can be assigned to the Wilton culture. The occurrence of pigmy tools in the Kitchen Middens and the peculiar custom of painting the burial stones laid on the bodies does however suggest a fairly close connection between some of the Kitchen Midden folk and the Wilton artists.

What we learn from a study of the art groups endorses these conclusions in a remarkable manner. The earlier series in Southern Rhodesia were painted in all probability by the first Neoanthropic invaders[2]. In the Union itself the Wilton people seemed to have developed a peculiar and not particularly beautiful style, whereas the artistic mantle fell on the folk belonging to the Smithfield culture. Why this was so and why the Wilton folk, who in Southern Rhodesia seem to have been

[1] Professor Schwarz in *Science Progress* for July 1926–7, Vol. I, suggests that the San Bushfolk were in the Sudan in predynastic Egyptian times. He even suggests that among the engravings found by Hassanein Bey at the oasis of Owenat there is a drawing of a San Bushman shooting an ostrich with a bow and arrow. Schwarz claims that Bushmen were known to the Egyptians of the Sixth Dynasty and earlier. He quotes the adventures of Her-Khuf, governor of Elephantine near Aswan, who went to an oasis which he calls Uhat (not so unlike Owenat!) and brought back with him a dwarf or "tenk." Even from the First Dynasty these dwarf people were in great demand. On the death of a king they were sacrificed as their dancing pleased the powers of the Underworld who then let through the Pharaoh lightly. Their dancing, too, was an attraction to the more important people of this world and the dwarfs were in demand for many purposes.

[2] Compare Bambata Cave (1) where a pre-Wilton industry occurs and also the earliest series of the paintings, and Nswatugi Cave where the earliest series does not occur, nor do any pre-Wilton industries.

the direct successors of the Neoanthropic artists, did not continue to paint rock-shelters in the central districts, but have only left us a degenerate art in the southern area, is unknown. It is a thousand pities that our knowledge of paintings in the north and north-eastern Transvaal is so meagre—just the region connecting the two artistic areas. Certain it is, however, that the Wilton culture in the extreme south of the continent is in a final stage of development and far more evolved than it is in Southern Rhodesia. It may be that in the course of time the Wilton folk in the new country had to a certain extent dropped their artistic tendencies.

So we see the story of South Africa as a series of migrations from the north drifting slowly into the country one after the other, and, having arrived, intermixing with each other and sometimes forming new local developments, the whole process continuing until quite recent times. This is what makes the archaeology of South Africa so interesting. It carries us down to the day before yesterday, and the whole country, although the cradle for a number of autochthonous growths, is in its broad aspects one gigantic, wonderfully stocked, museum of the past.

BIBLIOGRAPHY

(1) ARNOLD, Dr G. and Rev. NEVILLE JONES. "Notes on the Bushman Cave at Bambata, Matopos." *Proc. Rhodesia Scientific Association*, Vol. XVII, Part I, June 1918–1919.

(2) BREUIL, H. "Les peintures rupestres du bassin inférieur de l'Ebre. II. Les fresques à l'air libre de Cogul, province de Lérida (Catalogne)." *L'Anthropologie*, Tome XX, 1909.

(3) BREUIL, H. "Les peintures rupestres d'Espagne. III. Los Toricos d'Albarracin (Teruel)." *L'Anthropologie*, Tome XXII, 1911.

(4) BREUIL, H. "Les peintures rupestres d'Espagne. IV. Les Abris del Bosque à Alpéra (Albacete)." *L'Anthropologie*, Tome XXIII, 1912.

(5) BURKITT, M. C. *Prehistory*. 2nd edition, 1926.

(6) BURKITT, M. C. *Our Forerunners*. Home University Series.

(7) BROOM, R. "The evidence afforded by the Boskop Skull of a New Species of Primitive Man." *Anthr. Papers of the American Mus. of Nat. Hist.* Vol. XVIII, Part II, 1918.

(8) DART, R. A. "The Round Stone Culture of South Africa." *South African Journal of Science*, Vol. XXII, pp. 437–440, November, 1925.

(9) DART, R. A. "The Historical Succession of Cultural Impacts upon South Africa." *Nature*, March 21, 1925.

(10) DART, R. A. "Mammoths and Man in the Transvaal." *Nature*, December 10, 1927.

(11) DURAND, P., LAVAUDEN, L. et BREUIL, H. "Les peintures rupestres de la Grotte d'In-Ezzan." *L'Anthropologie*, Tome XXXVI, 1926.

(12) DU TOIT, A. L. *The Geology of South Africa*. Edinburgh, 1926.

(13) FITZSIMONS, F. W. "The Cliff Dwellers of Zitzikama." *South African Journal of Science*, Vol. XX, pp. 541–544, December, 1923.

(14) FITZSIMONS, F. W. "Cliff Dwellers of Zitzikama: Results of Recent Excavations." *South African Journal of Science*, Vol. XXIII, pp. 813–817, December, 1926.

(15) FROBENIUS, L. and OBERMAIER, H. *Hádschra Máktuba*. Munich, 1925.

(16) GOODWIN, A. J. H. *A Handbook to the Collections of Stone Implements* (South African Museum Guide Leaflet No. 2), August, 1926.

(17) GOODWIN, A. J. H. "South African Stone Implement Industries." *South African Journal of Science*, Vol. XXIII, pp. 784–788, December, 1926.

(18) GOODWIN, A. J. H. "The Hardy Collection of Stone Implements." *South African Journal of Science*, Vol. XXIII, pp. 826–832, December, 1926.

(19) GOODWIN, A. J. H. "The Montagu Cave." *Annals of the South African Museum*, Vol. XXIV, Part I.

(20) GOODWIN, A. J. H. "A Comparison between the Capsian and South African Stone Cultures." *Annals of the South African Museum*, Vol. XXIV, Part I; also "Capsian Affinities of South African Later Stone Age Culture." *South African Journal of Science*, Vol. XXII, pp. 428-436, November 1925.

(21) GOODWIN, A. J. H. "The Archaeology of the Vaal River Gravels." *Trans. Royal Society of South Africa*, Vol. XVI, Part I.

(22) HALL, R. N. and NEAL, W. G. *The Ancient Ruins of Rhodesia.* London, 1904.

(23) HALL, R. N. *Great Zimbabwe.* London, 1907.

(24) HARRISON, JANE. *Ancient Art and Ritual.* Home University Series.

(25) HEESE, C. H. T. D. "Notes on some ground and polished stone implements from the North-West Karroo." *South African Journal of Science*, Vol. XXIII, pp. 789-792, December, 1926.

(26) HEWITT, J. "On several Implements and Ornaments from Strandlooper sites in the Eastern Province." *South African Journal of Science*, Vol. XVIII, 1922.

(27) HEWITT, J. "On some stone implements from the Cape Province." *South African Journal of Science*, Vol. XXII, pp. 441-453, November, 1925.

(28) HEWITT, J. "Some peculiar elements in the Wilton Culture of the Eastern Province." *South African Journal of Science*, Vol. XXIII, pp. 901-904, December, 1926.

(29) HEWITT, J. and Rev. P. STAPLETON. "On some remarkable stone implements in the Albany Museum, Grahamstown." *South African Journal of Natural History*, Vol. V, pp. 23-38, December, 1925.

(30) HUSS, B. and Brother OTTO. "The origin of the bushmen paintings at the Kei River." *South African Journal of Science*, Vol. XXII, pp. 496-503, November, 1925.

(31) JOHNSON, J. P. *The Stone Implements of South Africa.* Second edition, Longmans, 1908.

(32) JOHNSON, J. P. *The Prehistoric Period in South Africa.* Second edition, Longmans, 1912.

(33) JONES, N. *The Stone Age in Rhodesia.* O. U. P., 1926.

(34) LAING, GORDON D. "A preliminary report on some Strandlooper skulls found at Zitzikama." *South African Journal of Science*, Vol. XXI, July 9, 1924.

(35) LAING, GORDON D. "A further report on the Zitzikama material." *South African Journal of Science*, Vol. XXII, pp. 455-457, November, 1925.

(36) LAMPLUGH, G. W. "Notes on the occurrence of Stone Implements in the valley of the Zambezi round Victoria Falls." *Journal of the Roy. Anthr. Inst. of Great Britain and Ireland*, Vol. XXXVI, 1906.

(37) MACRAE, F. B. "The Stone Age in Northern Rhodesia." *Nada, The Southern Rhodesia Native Affairs Department Annual*, 1926.

(38) MORGAN, J. de (and others). "Études sur les stations préhistorique, du Sud Tunisien." *Rev. de l'École d'Anthr.*, Tome XX, April 1910 *et seq.*

(39) OBERMAIER, H. "Las pinturas rupestres del Barranco de Valltorta (Castellón)." *Com. de Invest. Pal. y Prehist.*, Mem. num. 23, Madrid, 1919.

(40) PÉRINGUEY, L. "The Stone Ages of South Africa." *Annals of the South African Museum*, Vol. VIII.

(41) SCHAPERA, I. "A Preliminary consideration of the Relationship between the Hottentots and the Bushmen." *South African Journal of Science*, Vol. XXIII, pp. 833–866, December, 1926. Also "Some Stylistic Affinities of Bushman Art." *South African Journal of Science*, Vol. XXII, pp. 504–515, November, 1925.

(42) SCHOFIELD, J. F. "Zimbabwe: a Critical Examination of the Building Methods employed." *South African Journal of Science*, Vol. XXIII, 1926.

(43) SELIGMAN, C. G. "The Older Palaeolithic Age in Egypt." *Journ. of the Roy. Anthr. Inst. of Great Britain and Ireland*, Vol. LI, Jan.–June, 1921.

(44) SOLLAS, W. J. *Ancient Hunters*. Third edition, London, 1924.

(45) STAPLETON, Rev. P. (S.J.) "Note on a stone axe from Fort Hare." *Rec. Albany Mus.*, Vol. III.

(46) STAPLETON, Rev. P. (S.J.) and HEWITT, J. "Some Stone Implements from a Rock-Shelter at Howieson's Poort, near Grahamstown." *South African Journal of Science*, Vol. XXIV, pp. 574–587, December, 1927.

(47) STOW, G. W. *The Native Races of South Africa*. London, 1905.

(48) TONGUE, M. HELEN. *Bushman Paintings*. O. U. P., 1909.

(49) TAREL, R. "Gisements préhistoriques de l'oasis de Tabelbala." *Revue Anthropol.*, Tome XXIV, 1914.

(50) VAN RIET LOWE, C. "The Modder River man and his possible relation to the Smithfield Industry." *South African Journal of Science*, Vol. XXIII, 1926.

(51) WAYLAND, E. J. and SMITH, R. A. "Some primitive stone implements from Uganda." *Geol. Surv. Dept. Occas. Paper*, No. 1, 1923.

(52) ŽELÍZKO, I. V. *Felsgravierungen der Südafrikanischen Buschmänner*. Leipzig, 1925.

INDEX

Acheulean culture, 6, 60, 62, 70, 72
Africa, North, industries in, 69, 70, 84, 86. *See also* Fayum, Sahara, Tabelbala
Africa, South, history and prehistory in, 1, 14, 15, 16, ch. XI; classification of cultures and industries in, 16; geology and geography, ch. II; description of archaeological tour in, ch. III; industries of, chs. III–VI; prehistoric art in, chs. VII–IX
Afvallingskop, engravings at, 40, 104, 146, 150, Figs. XXVI–XXVIII
Alexandersfontein Pan, industries near, 34, 78, 97
Alicedale, Wilton industry, 46, 47
Aliwal North, paintings at, 43, 104, 133, 135
Antelope, in rock paintings, 118
Arrow-head, from Halfway House, 33, 104
Art, prehistoric, chs. VII–IX *passim.* *See also* Paintings, Engravings
Artefacts, defined, 2
Ashton, Cape Province, *see* Montagu Cave
Associated finds, evidence of, 13 ff., 113
Asturian culture, 6
Aurignacian culture, 6, 81
Azilian culture, 6

Baboon, in rock paintings, 135; in rock engravings, 150
Balls, stone, 64, Fig. VII, 1; bored, 92, 102, Fig. XVIII, 2
Bambata cave (Matopos), 17, 82, 126
Bantu, the, and rock paintings, 119, 124, 128, 131, 136, 138, 154; and Zimbabwe, 162, 163, 166
Barberton, paintings near, 133
Beads, ostrich egg, 90; Roman, 92; European trade, 105
Beatrice Road, painted rock-shelter, 117–8, Pl. IV
Black Kei River, the, 44, 138

Bleek, Miss, and Bushman paintings, 144
Bloemfontein, 38, 42; tool from, 70, Fig. X, 3
Bloemhof, mammoth teeth found near, 24
Boskop skull, the, viii, 52
Botha River, the, paintings near, 46
Bouwers drift, prehistoric site at, 45
Bows, in rock paintings, 119, 139, 140
Brakfontein, prehistoric sites near, 39–40, 42, 70; implements from, 70, 72, Fig. X, 1, 2, Fig. XVI, 2, Fig. XVII
Britstown, implements from, 51, 102
Broderick, E., of the Government Native Industrial School, 119, 121
Bronze Age, the, in Europe, 6
Buck, in rock paintings, 118, 122, 134, 135; in rock engravings, 149
Buffalo, in rock paintings, 118, 119, 122, 140; in rock engravings, 150
Bulawayo, industries near, 35–6; rock paintings near, 123
Burial stones, 106, Fig. XX, 1
Burins, at Howieson's Poort, 47–8, 81–2; Smithfield, 97, 98
Bushman Cave, at the "World's View," 124
Bushmen, the, and associated culture, 17, 25, 28, 33, 34, 36, 43, 46, 172, 173 *n.*; bored stones, 92; and Strandloopers, 105–6; paintings, 110, 152, 154, 158

Camp Siding, *see* Tylden
Campignian culture, 6, 66
Capsian culture, 6, 86, 170; implements, 96, 97
Cape Flats, implements from, Fig. XV, 1–10, 12–21, 23–28
Cape St Blaize, 49; cave at, 50
Cape Town, prehistoric sites near, 51–4, 93

Great Kei, paintings at, 138
Gwelo, industries at, 37–8

Halfway House, implements from, 33, 58, 104; engravings at, 149, 159
Hall, R. N., and Zimbabwe, 160
Hands, human, in rock paintings, 46, 152, 154, Pl. VII, Fig. XXIX
Hardy, Col., tools collected by, 86, 170
Harrismith, discoveries at, 92 *n.*
Heese, C. H. T. D., and Still Bay, 50; at Britstown, 51, 102
Heilbron, stone balls from, 64
Hermanus, implements from, 53, 108
Herschel, paintings at, 43, 104, 133
Hewitt, J., excavation by, 47, 81, 89
Horses, paintings of, 118
Howieson's Poort, rock-shelter at, 47; industry at, 81, 168, 170, Fig. XIII; and Still Bay, 88; rock painting at, Fig. XXIX, 4

Ice Age, the, 20; in Africa, 21
Impey, Dr, and painted rock-shelters, 36, 126, 127, 128
Impey's Cave, 126–8, Pl. II
Industry, defined, 2
Inyati River, the, 36; tools from, Fig. VIII, 2
Iram, painted rock-shelter at, 36, 126 ff.
Iron Age, the, in Europe, 6

Jacobsdal, engravings at, 40
Jansen, J., at Victoria West, 55
Johnson, J. P., on prehistoric cultures, 17
Jones, Neville, and Palaeolithic industries, 36, 47, 80, 82; at De Kiel Oost, 41, 97

Kafferkuils River, the, and Still Bay, 50, 84
Kannemeyer, Dr, at Smithfield, 93
Karroo, the, and Victoria West culture, 27, 29, 55. *See* Victoria West
Kempsie Glen, painted panel at, 128, Fig. XXI
Kenhardt, rock engravings, 145

Kenya, archaeology in, 18, 52, 81, 82, 84, 86, 168, 170, 172; obsidian implements from, Fig. XX, 1–6
Keurfontein, Smithfield industry near, 31
Kilgobbin Farm, rock paintings at, 136
Kimberley, and Smithfield industry, 32–4
Kitchen Midden culture, 6, 17, 105–8, 173; distribution, 28, 48–9, 50, 52; at Still Bay, 84
Klein Philippolis, industries at, 38–9; implements, Fig. XVII
Koffiefontein, prehistoric sites near, 40, 70
Kokwe River, the, implements from, 36
Koodoo, in rock paintings, 119, 122, 123, 125, 129, 130, Frontispiece *and* Fig. XXI

Ladismith, painted site near, 142
Lake Chrissie, paintings near, 133
Lamplugh, G. W., on Victoria Falls, 34
Laurel leaf tools, 13; in Still Bay industry, 84, 86, 170, Fig. XIV
Leakey, L. S. B., in Kenya, 18, 52, 81, 84, 86, 169, 170
Lebakwe district, the, implements from, 36
Levallois flakes, 58, 59, 76, 78
Lichtenberg, and river problems, 22–3; 38; implement from, 80
Lonely Mine Road, *see* Ematjeni River

Macrae, F. B., in N. Rhodesia, 18, 64
Magdalenian culture, in Europe, 6
Magic, and art, 110, 119–21
Maglemosean culture, in Europe, 6
Magosi culture, Uganda, 89, 172
Makumbi, rock paintings, 34, 111, 118, 121 ff., 132, Frontispiece *and* Pl. I
Mammoth, teeth of, from Bloemhof, 24, 167
Man, in rock paintings, 118, 119, 122, 123, 125, 126–8, 134, 135, 136, 138, 139, 140, Fig. XXI; engravings, 146

CPSIA information can be obtained at www.ICGtesting.com
Printed in the USA
BVOW011715081211

277885BV00001B/126/P